To Amelia,
and to my parents

Für Amelia,
und für meine Eltern

David Cohn

Young Spanish Architects
Junge spanische Architekten

Birkhäuser
Basel · Berlin · Boston

Translation
 Übersetzung

Andreas Simon, Berlin

Layout and cover design
 Gestaltung und Typografie

Martin Schack, Dortmund

Cover illustration
 Umschlagabbildung

María Fraile & Javier Revillo,
Trade Fair Exhibition Hall
Photo: Luis Asin

All illustrations were provided
by the architects, except where
noted otherwise.

Alle Abbildungen wurden von
den Architekten zur Verfügung
gestellt, sofern nicht anders
angegeben.

A CIP catalogue record for this
book is available from the Library
of Congress, Washington D.C.,
USA

Deutsche Bibliothek Cataloging-
in-Publication Data

Young Spanish architects =
Junge spanische Architekten /
David Cohn. – Basel ; Berlin ;
Boston : Birkhäuser, 2000

ISBN 3-7643-6043-7
ISBN 0-8176-6043-7

© 2000 Birkhäuser – Publishers
for Architecture, P.O.Box 133,
CH-4010 Basel, Switzerland

Printed on acid-free paper
produced from chlorine-free
pulp.

Printed in Germany

ISBN 3-7643-6043-7

ISBN 0-8176-6043-7

9 8 7 6 5 4 3 2 1

Contents
Inhalt

7 **Imagining Other Paradigms**
   Auf dem Weg zu neuen Paradigmen

20 Iñaki Ábalos & Juan Herreros, Madrid

28 Emilio Tuñón & Luis Moreno Mansilla, Madrid

38 María Fraile & Javier Revillo, Madrid

46 Juan Ignacio Mera, Madrid

54 Foreign Office Architects: Alejandro Zaera & Farshid Moussavi, London

62 Manuel Ruisánchez & Xavier Vendrell, Barcelona

70 Enric Batlle & Joan Roig, Barcelona

78 Rafael Aranda, Carme Pigem & Ramón Vilalta, Olot, Girona

86 Francisco Mangado, Pamplona

94 Fernando Tabuenca & Jesús Leache, Pamplona
    Eduardo de Miguel, Valencia

104 Jesús Irisarri & Guadalupe Piñera, Vigo

112 Ignacio Rubiño, Pura García Márquez, Luis Rubiño, Sevilla

120 Javier García-Solera & Alfredo Payá, Alicante

128 Manuel Feo, Las Palmas de Gran Canaria

136 **Biographies, Selected Works, Selected Bibliography**
     Biographien, Ausgewählte Werke, Auswahlbibliographie

Imagining Other Paradigms
Auf dem Weg zu neuen Paradigmen

For international observers who received their last major introduction to contemporary Spanish architecture in 1992, on the occasion of the Barcelona Olympics and the Seville Expo, the time has come to re-evaluate that portrait, incorporating the work of a new generation. Spain's recovery from the post-Olympic economic recession, which lasted roughly from 1992 to 1995, and the steady demand for new public buildings, largely driven by a process of decentralization and growth in Spain's regional autonomous governments and municipalities, together with incentives such as open competitions and special exhibitions, conferences and award programs, has permitted the generation of architects near or under 40 years of age to become a dynamic new presence over the past five years.

The events of 1992 marked the culmination of the euphoric, heroic period of Spain's transition to democratic government in the 1980s, following the death of Franco in 1975. Massive public investments in basic infrastructures, services and planned urban development during that period permitted the emergence of a vigorous architectural culture, protagonized by figures mainly born in the late 1930s and early 1940s, such as Rafael Moneo, Esteve Bonell, Juan Navarro, and Guillermo Vázquez Consuegra, whose work became a symbol of Spain's optimistic new spirit. [1]

This architectural renewal found its sources in the fragile currents of the modern tradition that had been re-introduced to an isolated Spain in the late 1950s, updated through scattered contacts with other countries (in particular, the work of Scandinavians such as Aalto, Jacobsen and Utzon, and Bruno Zevi's Organicism in the 1960s), and passed on to the generation of 1992 by older teachers such as Alejandro de la Sota and Francisco J. Sáenz de Oíza in Madrid, and José A. Coderch and Oriol Bohigas in Barcelona. Thus, at a time when the basic tenets and assumptions of the modern movement were undergoing a profound revision in the rest of Europe and the United States, in Spain a neglected modernism, free of the negative associations it had accumulated elsewhere, was revindicated as an instrument and symbol of reason, progress and political change.

Nach der letzten bedeutenden Einführung in die zeitgenössische spanische Architektur von 1992 aus Anlaß der Olympischen Spiele und der Expo in Sevilla ist die Zeit gekommen, das Bild mit den Arbeiten einer neuen Generation aufzufrischen. Die wirtschaftliche Erholung Spaniens nach der Rezession, die den Olympischen Spielen folgte und etwa von 1992 bis 1995 andauerte, sowie die beständige Nachfrage nach neuen öffentlichen Gebäuden, weitgehend angetrieben durch den Dezentralisierungs- und Wachstumsprozeß der autonomen Regionalregierungen und Kommunen, erlaubten in den letzten fünf Jahren zusammen mit Anreizen wie offenen Wettbewerben, besonderen Ausstellungen, Kongressen und neuen Architekturpreisen der neuen Generation von Architekten, die heute um die 40 Jahre oder jünger sind, zu einer dynamischen neuen Kraft zu werden.

1992 war der Kulminationspunkt der euphorischen, heroischen Phase von Spaniens Wandel zur Demokratie in den 80er Jahren, nach dem Tod Francos 1975. Massive öffentliche Investitionen in die grundlegende Infrastruktur, öffentliche Dienste und gezielte Stadtentwicklung während dieser Zeit schufen eine lebendige Architekturkultur, deren Vertreter vor allem in den späten 30er und frühen 40er Jahren geboren wurden, darunter Rafael Moneo, Esteve Bonell, Juan Navarro und Guillermo Vázquez Consuegra, deren Arbeiten zum Symbol des neuen, optimistischen Spanien wurden.[1]

Diese architektonische Erneuerung speiste sich aus den wechselnden Strömungen der modernen Tradition, die in einem zuvor isolierten Spanien in den 50er Jahren wiederaufgenommen und durch vereinzelte Kontakte zu anderen Ländern (besonders Skandinavier wie Aalto, Jacobsen und Utzon sowie Bruno Zevis Organizismus in den 60er Jahren) aufgefrischt und an die jüngere Generation von 1992 durch ältere Lehrer wie Alejandro de la Sota und Francisco J. Sáenz de Oíza in Madrid sowie José A. Coderch und Oriol Bohigas in Barcelona weitergegeben wurden. So wurde zu einer Zeit, als im übrigen Europa und in den USA die grundlegenden Lehrmeinungen und Annahmen der modernen Architektur einer tiefgreifenden Revision unterzogen wurden, diese in Spanien, wo sie vernachlässigt worden war, als Instrument und Symbol von Vernunft, Fortschritt und politischem Wandel verteidigt.

When the generation of 1992 incorporated neo-rationalist and postmodern concerns in their work, they did so in a spirit of continuity rather than rupture with the modern tradition. Taking the Miesian clarity of Alejandro de la Sota's work as a starting point, for example, Juan Navarro would add a poetics of experiential phenomenology, while Manuel Gallego would locate De la Sota's abstract technique in the specific landscape and culture of Galicia. And to the radical eclecticism of Sáenz de Oíza, product of a restless avantgarde spirit of experiment and speculation, Rafael Moneo would add a dimension of historic reflection and contextual dialogue between the traditional and contemporary city, an approach taken up in similar terms by Seville architects Antonio Cruz and Antonio Ortiz.

A sense of continuity with the modern project was also evident in the Madrid public housing of Manuel de las Casas, the Equipo Auia group,[2] Mariano Bayón and others, whose combination of innovative type forms and unit plans with new concepts of urban space were a direct continuation of Madrid's long tradition in housing research, dating back to Arturo Soria's Linear City at the beginning of the century, and including the emergency settlements of the 1950s where De la Sota and Sáenz de Oíza got their start.

In Barcelona, Oriol Bohigas was the most important link between modernism and new theoretical developments. The modernist practice of forming avant-garde associations around a manifesto of theoretical principles, as exemplified by Barcelona's GATEPAC group in the 1930s or the Grupo R of the 1950s, of which Bohigas was a leading member as a young man, was echoed in the alliance of politicians and architects Bohigas helped forge to implement Barcelona's famed urban planning program. At the same time, as the chief conceptual designer of the program and later of the Olympic Village, Bohigas assimilated the neo-rationalist critique of modern city planning, producing a hybrid of modern and traditional ideas which stands today as probably the most advanced urban theory put into practice by a city government.

The large group of architects who received commissions under the Barcelona program tended to be split more clearly than their other Spanish colleagues into postmodern and modern stylistic camps. Those architects with stronger international horizons and contacts, such as Ricardo Bofill, Oscar Tusquets and Lluís Clotet, were more inclined towards a posture of rupture with the modern tradition (as was the case with Basque architects José Ignacio Linazasoro and Miguel Garay in San Sebastián). In the other camp, the apparent restrictions of a more local field of reference often led to what for an outsider are more original and intriguing works, more opaque to conventional readings. Esteve Bonell, former partners Jordi Garcés and Enric Sòria, José Llinás, and

Als die Generation von 1992 neorationalistische und postmoderne Einflüsse in ihre Werke aufnahm, tat sie dies in einem Geist der Kontinuität, nicht des Bruchs mit der modernen Tradition. Der Klarheit der Arbeiten von Alejandro de la Sota, ihrerseits inspiriert von Mies van der Rohe, fügte etwa Juan Navarro eine Poetik experimenteller Phänomenologie hinzu, während Manuel Gallego De la Sotas abstrakte Technik in die besondere Landschaft und Kultur Galiciens übertrug. Und den radikalen Eklektizismus von Sáenz de Oíza, Produkt einer rastlosen, avantgardistischen Experimentierfreude, bereicherte Rafael Moneo um eine Dimension historischer Reflexion und des kontextuellen Dialogs zwischen traditioneller und zeitgenössischer Stadt, ein Ansatz, der in ähnlicher Weise von den Architekten Antonio Cruz und Antonio Ortiz in Sevilla aufgenommen wurde.

Ein Gefühl der Kontinuität mit dem Projekt der Moderne ist auch in den öffentlichen Madrider Wohnbauten von Manuel de las Casas, der Gruppe Equipo Auia[2], Mariano Bayón und anderen spürbar, deren Kombination innovativer typologischer Formen und Grundrißgestaltungen von Wohneinheiten mit neuen Konzepten des urbanen Raums eine direkte Fortführung der langen Madrider Tradition des experimentellen Wohnhausbaus darstellte, die auf Arturo Sorias „lineare Stadt" und die Anfänge des Jahrhunderts sowie die neuen Siedlungen in den 50er Jahren zurückgeht, mit denen De la Sota und Sáenz de Oíza ihre Karriere begannen.

In Barcelona war Oriol Bohigas der wichtigste Vermittler zwischen moderner Architektur und neuen theoretischen Entwicklungen. Die moderne Praxis, avantgardistische Assoziationen um ein Manifest theoretischer Prinzipien zu formen, wie es die Gruppe GATEPAC aus Barcelona in den 30er Jahren oder die Gruppe R, in der Bohigas als junger Mann ein führendes Mitglied war, in den 50er Jahren beispielhaft vorführte, fand in der Allianz von Politikern und Architekten zur Verwirklichung des berühmten Stadtplanungsprogramms Barcelonas, die Bohiga schmieden half, ihr Echo. Gleichzeitig Chef der konzeptionellen Gestaltung des Programms und später des Olympischen Dorfs, nahm Bohigas die neorationalistische Kritik der modernen Stadtplanung auf und schuf eine Mischung aus modernen und traditionellen Ideen, die heute zur vielleicht fortschrittlichsten urbanen Theorie geworden ist, die von einer Stadt in die Praxis umgesetzt wird.

Durch die große Gruppe von Architekten, die im Rahmen des Stadtplanungsprogramms von Barcelona Aufträge erhielten, verlief eine klarere Trennungslinie zwischen postmodernen und modernen Gestaltungsansätzen als bei anderen spanischen Kollegen. Diese Architekten mit ihrem internationalen Horizont und ihrem breiteren Spektrum an internationalen Kontakten, wie Ricardo Bofill, Oscar Tusquets und Lluís Clotet, neigten stärker zu einem Bruch mit der modernen Tradition (wie auch die baskischen Architekten José Ignacio Linazasoro

the radical minimalists Alberto Viaplana and Helio Piñón are prominent among this group. Perhaps the architects who best managed to maintain a wider perspective were Elías Torres and José A. Martínez Lapeña, whose work was at the same time in clear continuity with the regionally inflected modernism of Coderch, as well as the modernist currents from Madrid's master teachers.

The factors that contributed to the formation of this remarkable group have also been decisive for the succeeding generation. Virtually all the architects presented here teach in schools of architecture, which function as centers of the architectural community and provide a minimal income to fledgling practitioners. As critic Juan Daniel Fullaondo first proposed in the 1960s, it remains valid today to speak of a "School of Madrid" and a "School of Barcelona" as terms of inter-generational identity, a common design culture or outlook, and an *esprit de corps*. While Madrid and Barcelona are still the two main poles of reference, schools in Pamplona, Seville, Las Palmas, La Coruña and elsewhere, many organized in the last 15 years, are setting the groundwork for new regional identities. In addition, the colleges of architecture, powerful gremial associations which operate in every major city, play an important role in promoting quality design through the sponsorship of regional magazines, publications, exhibitions and other forums.

Spain's schools of architecture are also worth noting for their rigorous training in technical issues of structure and construction, a consequence of the wide responsibilities Spanish architects have traditionally had in these areas. This technical and practical orientation in an academic setting of master-student relations and theoretical speculation has contributed decisively to the distinctive character of Spanish architecture, its unique mixture of technical and intellectual rigor.

Moves to bring Spanish architectural education into conformity with European Community standards, which have reduced some of its more stringent requirements in recent years, have come too late to affect the generation considered here. The broad social changes accompanying the transition to democracy have had an impact, however, making this the first group of Spanish architects to include an important number of women.

Despite this common background and context, oedipal tensions do in fact separate the architects of the new generation from their mentors. They have become the vehicle in Spain for some of the new developments appearing in other parts of Europe in the 1990s. As part of a general pendular movement away from the postmodern figuration of the 1980s, most of Spain's young architects have gravitated to-

Fraile & Revillo
Trade Fair Exhibition Hall, Zamora
Messehalle

und Miguel Garay in San Sebastián). Im anderen Lager führten die scheinbaren Restriktionen eines lokaleren Bezugshorizonts häufig zu Arbeiten, die aus der Sicht eines Außenstehenden origineller und faszinierender waren und sich nicht so leicht einer konventionellen Interpretation erschlossen. Esteve Bonell, die ehemaligen Partner Jordi Garcés und Enric Sòria, José Llinás und die radikalen Minimalisten Alberto Viaplana und Helio Piñón sind bedeutende Vertreter dieser Gruppe. Vielleicht gehören Elías Torres und José A. Martínes Lapeña zu jenen Architekten, denen es am besten gelang, eine breitere Perspektive zu bewahren. Ihre Arbeiten zeigten eine klare Kontinuität sowohl zum regional gefärbten Modernismus eines Coderch wie zu den modernistischen Strömungen der Madrider Meisterlehrer.

Die Faktoren, die zur Bildung dieser bemerkenswerten Gruppe von Architekten beitrugen, waren auch für die folgende Generation ausschlaggebend. Praktisch alle Architekten, die hier präsentiert werden, lehren an Architekturschulen, die als Zentren der Architekturgemeinde dienen und jungen Architekten ein minimales Einkommen sichern. Bereits in den 60er Jahren sprach der Architekturkritiker Juan Daniel Fullaondo von einer „Madrider Schule" und einer „Schule von Barcelona" im Sinne einer generationsübergreifenden Identität, einer gemeinsamen Gestaltungskultur oder Anschauung und eines Korpsgeistes dieser Institutionen, und dies bleibt auch heute noch richtig. Während Madrid und Barcelona immer noch die beiden Hauptbezugspunkte bleiben, legen Schulen in Pamplona, Sevilla, Las Palmas, La Coruña und anderswo, von denen viele sich in den letzten 15 Jahren formierten, die Grundlagen für neue regionale Identitäten. Darüber hinaus spielen die Architekturkollegien, einflußreiche Gremien, die es in jeder großen Stadt gibt, eine wichtige Rolle bei der Verbesserung der Gestaltungsqualität durch die Förderung regionaler Magazine, durch Veröffentlichungen, Ausstellungen und andere Foren.

Bemerkenswert ist auch das Gewicht, das Spaniens Architekturschulen auf die technische Ausbildung in Statik und Bautechnik legen, eine Folge der breiten Verantwortlichkeit, die spanische Architekten traditionell in diesen Bereichen hatten.

wards a more minimalist modernism, with affinities to that of Herzog and De Meuron, Dominique Perrault, Peter Zumthor and others, who often draw on the analytic procedures and formal rigor of contemporary art.

Other Spaniards, most notably the London-based Alejandro Zaera of Foreign Office Architects and the Madrid team of Federico Soriano and Dolores Palacios, have taken up a more theory-driven and experimental approach to design, which looks to contemporary cultural criticism, advanced mathematics and the like. The two currents are not mutually exclusive; elements of both are found in the writings and designs of Madrid architects Iñaki Ábalos and Juan Herreros. Finally, there are a number of young architects whose work is more difficult to classify, who for a variety of reasons have set out on more independent paths, such as Manuel Feo and his group in the Canary Islands, Jesús Irisarri and Guadalupe Piñera in Galicia, and the studio of Aranda, Pigem and Vilalta in Olot, Girona.

The oedipal thrust in the new generation's swing towards minimalism is nicely captured by the Madrid-based team of María Fraile and Javier Revillo when they declare, in their project statement for the Zamora Trade Fair Pavilion, their intention to "annul singularity, in so far as it is possible, and the figuration of architectural elements, to dilute and neutralize them in favor of the general space." In conversation, Fraile and Revillo include in this visceral rejection of singularity all the leading architects of the previous generation, from Isozaki and Gehry to Moneo and Siza.

When given the opportunity, members of the older generation have received this new tendency with matching hostility. In a presentation of new Spanish and Portuguese architects in Salamanca in October 1998, which was directed by Siza and Moneo, projects by Fraile and Revillo, Javier García Solera, Alfredo Payá and others were loudly denounced by older architects in the audience as "boxy," "unimaginative" and other epithets. One would have to go back to the early success of Enric Miralles and Carmen Pinos in Barcelona to find a similar sense of alarm among established figures.

The works that can be grouped within the minimalist tendency, though they share similarities with other European

Diese technische und praktische Orientierung in einer akademischen Umgebung, die von der Beziehung zwischen Meisterlehrer und Student geprägt ist, hat entscheidend zum besonderen Charakter der spanischen Architektur beigetragen, zu ihrer einzigartigen Mischung technischer und intellektueller Strenge.

Maßnahmen, mit denen einige der strengeren Anforderungen in jüngeren Jahren reduziert wurden, um die spanische Architekturlehre den Standards der Europäischen Union anzupassen, kamen zu spät, um die Generation, der hier unser Augenmerk gilt, noch zu berühren. Der breite soziale Wandel, der den Übergang zur Demokratie begleitete, hatte jedoch seine Auswirkungen: Dies ist die erste Generation spanischer Architekten, zu der eine bedeutende Zahl von Frauen gehört.

Trotz des gemeinsamen Hintergrunds und Kontextes ist das Verhältnis zwischen der neuen Generation und ihren Mentoren nicht ohne Spannungen. Sie sind heute in Spanien zum Vehikel für einige der neuen Entwicklungen geworden, die in den 90er Jahren in anderen Teilen Europas auftauchten. Im Rahmen einer Pendelbewegung weg von der postmodernen Gestaltung der 80er Jahre wandten sich die meisten jungen spanischen Architekten einer minimalistischeren modernen Architektur zu, die Affinitäten zu Herzog & De Meuron, Dominique Perrault, Peter Zumthor und anderen aufweist, Architekten, die häufig auf die analytische Vorgehensweise und formale Strenge zeitgenössischer Kunst zurückgreifen.

Andere Spanier, besonders der in London arbeitende Alejandro Zaera von Foreign Office Architects und das Madrider Team von Federico Soriano und Dolores Palacios, haben sich einen theoriebetonteren und experimentelleren Gestaltungsansatz zu eigen gemacht, der sich an zeitgenössischer Kulturkritik, höherer Mathematik und ähnlichem orientiert. Die beiden Strömungen schließen sich gegenseitig nicht aus; Elemente beider finden sich in den Schriften und Entwürfen der Madrider Architekten Iñaki Ábalos und Juan Herreros. Schließlich gibt es eine Reihe junger Architekten, deren Werk schwieriger zu klassifizieren ist und die aus einer Reihe von Gründen unabhängigere Wege beschritten haben, wie Manuel Feo und seine Gruppe auf den Kanarischen Inseln, Jesús Irisarri und Guadalupe Piñera in Galicien und das Büro Aranda, Pigem und Vilalta in Olot, Girona.

Die Kritik an der älteren Generation, die in der minimalistischen Neigung der neuen zum Ausdruck kommt, zeigt sich sehr schön an den Arbeiten des Madrider Teams von María Fraile und Javier Revillo, wenn sie in ihrer Projektbeschreibung für den Messepavillon von Zamora ihre Absicht erklären, „Einzigartigkeit, so weit dies möglich ist, und die Formgebung architektonischer Elemente aufzuheben, sie zugunsten des allgemeinen Raums verschwimmen zu lassen und zu neutralisieren". Mit dieser instinktiven Ablehnung von Einzigartigkeit

projects, also maintain important differences. Designs such as the Zamora Trade Fair Pavilion, Ábalos and Herreros' Gordillo House, the Marbella Sports Pavilion by Ruisánchez and Vendrell, and Francisco Mangado's Zuasti Golf Club have much in common with the industrial projects of Herzog & De Meuron, for example: in their use of simple shed forms with repetitive expressed structures and sophisticated lightweight skins; in their careful, often Miesian proportions; and in their interest in the dialogue of luminosity, texture and material sensuality with the abstract play of planar surface and spatial volume.

But these similarities bring into relief subtle but fundamental differences. The Swiss architects' use of cladding materials such as copper strips, wood planks or rubble stonework is redolent of certain works of minimalist sculpture, in

Francisco Mangado
Zuasti Country Club,
Señorio de Zuasti

that it undercuts the functioning of a conventional formal language by emphasizing the sheer physicality and natural properties of the materials, a technique that can seem affectlessly direct at one moment and mystically "beyond language" in the next.

In comparison, the Spanish projects engage in a less polarized dialectic, which centers on the concrete question of construction technique rather than the abstract question of language. Their raw material is the manufacturers' catalog of parts, the assembly process, the detail, the building as a hands-on, craftsmanlike process of design and construction. If the work of the Swiss architects reminds us of the enigmatic boxes of Donald Judd, the Spanish projects take as their starting point the contemporary landscape of utilitarian building. And if the Swiss projects suggest Heideggerian issues of language, being and authenticity, the Spanish projects combine a realism of limited means and the imaginative potentiation of those means through the "enlightenment" of reason, that is to say, via the analytic methods and vocabulary of modern architecture.

In the Zamora Trade Fair Pavilion, this combination of realism and a modernist humanism is particularly clear. We note the bare coldness of the exposed concrete floors, the

wenden sich Fraile und Revillo, wie sie in einem Gespräch betonten, gegen alle führenden Architekten der vorangehenden Generation, von Isozaki und Gehry bis Moneo und Siza.

Wo sich die Gelegenheit bot, bedachten Mitglieder der älteren Generation diese neue Tendenz mit vergleichbarer Feindseligkeit. Bei einer Präsentation neuer spanischer und portugiesischer Architekten in Salmanca im Oktober 1998, die von Siza und Moneo geleitet wurde, belegten ältere Architekten im Publikum Projekte von Fraile und Revillo, Javier García Solera, Alfredo Payá und anderen offen mit Wörtern wie „schachtelartig", „phantasielos" und ähnlichen Ausdrücken. Man muß schon bis zum frühen Erfolg von Enric Miralles und Carmen Pinos in Barcelona zurückgehen, um eine vergleichbare Alarmstimmung unter den etablierten Architekten zu finden.

Die Arbeiten, die zur minimalistischen Richtung gezählt werden können, weisen jedoch bedeutende Unterschiede auf, wenn sie auch Ähnlichkeiten zu anderen europäischen Projekten zeigen. Entwürfe wie der Messepavillon in Zamora, das Gordillo-Haus von Ábalos und Herreros, der Sportpavillon von Marbella von Ruisánchez und Vendrell sowie Francisco Mangados Zuasti Golfclub haben zum Beispiel viel mit den Industriebauten von Herzog & De Meuron gemein: mit ihrem Einsatz einfacher Sägedachformen mit sich wiederholenden, offen sichtbaren Gerüsten und ausgeklügelten leichten Gebäudehäuten; in den sorgsam gewählten, häufig auf Mies van der Rohe verweisenden Proportionen; und in ihrem Interesse für den Dialog von Lichtdurchlässigkeit, Textur und der sinnlichen Qualität des Materials mit dem Spiel glatter Flächen und räumlichen Volumina.

Doch diese Ähnlichkeiten lassen auch subtile, aber grundlegende Unterschiede zu Tage treten. Der Einsatz von Fassadenverkleidungen wie Kupferbändern, Holzplatten oder Bruchsteinmauerwerk bei Schweizer Architekten erinnert an bestimmte minimalistische Skulpturen: Die Funktionsweise einer konventionellen Formensprache wird durch die Betonung der reinen Körperhaftigkeit und natürlichen Eigenschaften der Materialien unterlaufen, eine Technik, die manchmal emotionslos direkt wirkt, ein andermal jede Formensprache mystisch zu überschreiten scheint.

Im Vergleich dazu weisen die spanischen Projekte eine weniger polarisierte Dialektik auf, die stärker auf konkrete Fragen der Bautechnik als auf abstrakte Fragen der Architektursprache ausgerichtet ist. Ihr Rohmaterial ist der Katalog des Baustoffhändlers, der Montageprozeß, das Detail, das Gebäude als handgreiflicher und handwerklicher Gestaltungs- und Bauprozeß. Wo uns die Arbeiten der Schweizer Architekten an die enigmatischen Schachteln von Donald Judd erinnern, fußen die spanischen Projekte auf der zeitgenössischen Landschaft von Zweckbauten. Und wo die Schweizer Projekte um Heideggersche Themen der Sprache, des Seins und der Authentizität kreisen, verbinden die spanischen Projekte einen Realismus

disarming directness of the steel I-section columns and catalog trusses, and the inhospitable roughness of the galvanized and corrugated metal cladding sheets. But as we climb
the ramp of the podium and enter the building, we are liter-
ally elevated and enlarged by the scale and proportions, by
the spare, rhythmic repetition of elements, the quality of the
natural light, and the absence of incident, the spatial silence
that surrounds every human movement and gesture.

The young Spaniards' focus on building technique, their
most original contribution to European minimalism, comes
from the teachings of De la Sota. What makes De la Sota so
intriguing for the new minimalists is his effort, particularly
in later works such as the León Post Office (1981), to make
the building appear to be a direct manifestation of construction technique and functional program, without any visible
design intention or expressive agenda. This effort to cloak
aesthetic ambition in technical terms gives his work an elu-
sive inner intensity, which has become the riddle whose se-
cret many young architects seek to unlock through their own
designs, raising their work above simple functionalist or formalist formulas.

De la Sota's approach to design has been given a theoretical armature and presented in contemporary European forums by Ábalos and Herreros, who propose in works such as
the Gordillo House that "technique can reveal to the most

alert the mechanisms with which to imagine another paradigm." Recently, however, they have concluded that more
than pure technique is required to imaginatively project or
inhabit a building, and they are experimenting with more
subjective categories of engagement, although with the
same cool distance. Thus, the silkscreened facades of their
prototype "A&H" prefabricated houses apply lessons from
American Pop Art, and their urban designs explore ways of
destructuring space for more open social interactions.

De la Sota's pose of invisibility has been taken up in different terms by Luis Mansilla and Emilio Tuñón, who form
another major young studio in Madrid. While they are active
teachers, writers and speakers, they avoid direct comments

begrenzter Mittel mit der phantasievollen Potenzierung dieser Mittel durch die „aufklärerische" Vernunft, das heißt ver-
mittels der analytischen Methoden und des Vokabulars der
modernen Architektur.

Beim Messepavillon von Zamora wird diese Verbindung von
Realismus und modernistischem Humanismus besonders
deutlich. Wir bemerken die nackte Kälte der sichtbaren Beton-
böden, die entwaffnende Direktheit der Doppel-T-Stahlstüt-
zen und handelsüblichen Träger und die ungastliche Rauheit
der verzinkten Wellblechpaneele der Außenverkleidung. Doch
steigt man die Rampe des Podiums hoch und betritt das Gebäude, fühlt man sich durch die Dimensionen und Proportionen, die sparsame, rhythmische Wiederholung von Elementen, die Qualität des natürlichen Lichts und die Abwesenheit
des Zufälligen, die räumlich Ruhe, die jede menschliche Bewegung und Geste umhüllt, geradezu emporgehoben und grö-
ßer.

Die Konzentration der jungen Spanier auf die Bautechnik,
ihr originellster Beitrag zum europäischen Minimalismus, verdankt sich dem Einfluß De la Sotas. Was De la Sota für die
neuen Minimalisten so faszinierend macht, ist sein besonders
in späteren Werken wie dem Postamt von León (1981) deutlich werdendes Bemühen, das Gebäude als direkte Manifestation der Bautechnik und des funktionalen Programms erscheinen zu lassen, ohne eine sichtbare Gestaltungsabsicht oder
Ausdrucksintention. Dieses Bemühen, ästhetische Intention
hinter technischen Mitteln zu verstecken, gibt seinem Werk
eine schwer faßliche innere Intensität. Das Rätsel dieser Intensität versuchen viele junge Architekten ihren eigenen Entwürfen einzuverleiben, indem sie über schlichte funktionalisti-
sche oder formalistische Formeln hinausstreben.

Ábalos und Herreros haben De la Sotas Gestaltungsansatz
theoretisch verankert und ihn auf zeitgenössischen europäischen Foren präsentiert. In ihren Werken wie dem Gordillo-
Haus streben sie danach, „die Mechanismen, die ein anderes
Paradigma vorstellbar machen, für die aufmerksamsten Beobachter in der Technik offenbar werden" zu lassen. Kürzlich
kamen sie jedoch zu dem Schluß, daß mehr als Technik erfor-

about their own work, and their designs cannily evade obvious classification. Their working method, adopted largely from Rafael Moneo's, is based on an unpremeditated "take" or analysis of the problem at hand, interpreted through the prism of their evolving formal preoccupations. Observers can find a tension between tectonic form and representation similar to that in Moneo's work, and densely-packed compositions of highly articulated, machine-like elements, often working in section, that could have been developed from James Stirling.

Affinities with De la Sota and Moneo are visible in many other projects featured here. For Barcelona architects Enric Battle and Joan Roig, the connection to De la Sota comes via

the enthusiastic teaching of J. A. Martínez Lapeña, and the personal interpretations given his legacy by local architects Viaplana and Piñón and Pep Llinás. For Manuel Ruisánchez and Xavier Vendrell, who talk about finding the "mala leche" or hard-core character of each problem, the connection to Moneo comes from Moneo's former student Elías Torres, and Moneo's years of teaching in Barcelona.

Through slightly more indirect channels, the Madrid ethos of problem-oriented, non-stylistic design has taken firm root around the Navarra School of Architecture in Pamplona, where Javier Carvajal, a noted Organic-period Madrid architect, taught in his later years. In addition to Francisco Mangado, Eduardo de Miguel (recently relocated to Valencia), Fernando Tabuenca and Jesús Leache, we should mention the partnership in nearby Vitoria of Roberto Ercilla and Miguel Ángel Campo, who were born in the early 1950s, and the team of Miguel Ángel Alonso and Rufino Hernández. The Pamplona School has recently taken the lead over San Sebastián, the other major school of architecture in northern Spain, which was influential in the 1980s but has remained identified with neo-rationalism.

Within this general minimalist orbit we should also place Javier García-Solera and his building for the University of Alicante Business School, with its straight-forward use of precast concrete panels; the sharply-focused public housing

derlich ist, um ein Gebäude phantasievoll zu entwerfen oder zu bewohnen, und experimentieren nun mit subjektiveren Kategorien, wenngleich sie dabei die gleiche kühle Distanz bewahren. So machen sie mit den Siebdruckfassaden ihres vorgefertigten Prototyphauses „A&H" Anleihen bei amerikanischer Pop Art, und ihre Stadtentwürfe erkunden Wege, den Raum für eine offene soziale Interaktion zu destrukturieren.

Luis Mansilla und Emilio Tuñon, ein weiteres bedeutendes junges Architekturbüro in Madrid, haben De la Sotas „Tarnkappenarchitektur" mit anderen Mitteln aufgenommen. Obwohl sie aktiv lehren, schreiben und Vorträge halten, vermeiden sie direkte Kommentare über ihre eigenen Werke, und ihre Entwürfe entziehen sich geschickt einer leichten Klassifizierbarkeit. Ihre Arbeitsmethode, die weitgehend von Rafael Moneo übernommen ist, beruht auf einer vorurteilsfreien „Aufnahme" oder Analyse des jeweiligen Problems, das dann durch das Prisma ihrer sich entwickelnden formalen Ziele interpretiert wird. Betrachter finden ähnlich wie bei Moneos Arbeiten eine Spannung zwischen tektonischer Form und Darstellung sowie verdichtete Kompositionen stark gegliederter, häufig im Profil sichtbarer maschinenartiger Elemente, die von James Stirling stammen könnten.

Affinitäten zu De la Sota und Moneo lassen sich in vielen anderen Projekten erkennen, die hier präsentiert werden. Für die Architekten Enric Battle und Joan Roig ergab sich die Verbindung zu De la Sota durch die enthusiastische Lehre von José A. Martínez Lapeña und die persönlichen Interpretationen, die sein Erbe durch die örtlichen Architekten Viaplana und Piñón und Pep Llináns erfuhr. Für Manuel Ruisánchez und Xavier Vendrell, die davon sprechen, den innersten Wesenskern jedes Problems zu finden, stellte sich die Verbindung zu Moneo über dessen ehemaligen Studenten Elías Torres und Moneos Dozentenjahre in Barcelona her.

Durch etwas indirektere Kanäle hat das Madrider Ethos eines problemorientierten, nicht-stilisierten Entwerfens in der Architekturschule von Pamplona feste Wurzel geschlagen, wo Javier Carvajal, ein bekannter Madrider Architekt aus der Phase der organischen Architektur, in seinen späteren Jahren lehr-

of Madrid-based Juan Ignacio Mera; and the intimately-scaled work of García Márquez, Rubiño and Rubiño in Seville, who, together with other young local designers, are beginning to form a distinctive Seville School around the offices of Cruz and Ortiz and Guillermo Vázquez Consuegra.

In a similar vein but with different conceptual premises, Aranda, Pigem and Vilalta of Olot, Girona bring the sleek, quirky intensity of industrial product design to their pared-down buildings. And in the Alicante University Museum, Al-

Batlle & Roig
Royal Automotive Club, Barcelona
Königlicher Automobilclub

Rubiño, García Márquez & Rubiño
Public Housing, Los Palacios
Soziale Wohnbauten

fredo Payá takes a more metaphysical approach, condensing the physical details of construction into a handful of abstract metaphoric relations, a strategy which recalls the work of Madrid architect and teacher Alberto Campo Baeza, and the religious chapels of Tadao Ando.

Among the handful of young Spanish architects who have resisted the powerful current of the new minimalism, the case of Alejandro Zaera is noteworthy as an experiment in establishing a truly global practice. Zaera first emerged while a young student in Madrid as a contributor to the influential journal *El Croquis*, founded in the early 1980s by two architects of the new generation, Fernando Márquez and Richard Levene. He used his studies at Harvard, where Moneo was Dean, and his two-year apprenticeship in the Rotterdam studio of Rem Koolhaas, to broaden his architectural horizons to an international scale. With his Iranian-born British wife Farshid Moussavi, he is now a Unit Master at London's Architectural Association. Thus, like Ricardo Bofill, Santiago Calatrava and Enric Miralles, he combines a

te. Neben Francisco Mangado, Eduardo de Miguel (jüngst nach Valencia umgezogen), Fernando Tabuenca und Jesús Leache sollten wir das Gemeinschaftsbüro von Roberto Ercilla und Miguel Ángel Campo (geboren Anfang der 50er Jahre) im nahen Vitoria erwähnen sowie das Team von Miguel Ángel Alonso und Rufino Hernández. Die Schule von Pamplona hat seit kurzem der Schule von San Sebastián, der anderen großen Architekturschule Nordspaniens, die in den 80er Jahren einflußreich war, deren Name aber mit dem Neorationalismus verbunden bleibt, den Rang abgelaufen.

Innerhalb dieses allgemeinen minimalistischen Orbits sollten wir auch Javier García-Solera und sein Gebäude für die Business School der Universität von Alicante mit seiner offenen Verwendung vorgefertigter Betonpaneele sehen; die scharf fokussierten öffentlichen Wohnbauten des Madriders Juan Ignacio Mera; sowie die fein dimensionierten Arbeiten von García Márquez, Rubiño und Rubiño in Sevilla, die zusammen mit anderen jungen Entwerfern die Fundamente einer charakteristischen Schule von Sevilla um die Architekturbüros von Cruz und Ortiz sowie Guillermo Vázquez Consuegra gelegt haben.

In ähnlicher Weise, jedoch mit anderen konzeptionellen Prämissen, verleihen Aranda, Pingem und Vilalta aus Olot, Girona, ihren bescheidenen Gebäuden die glatte, eigenwillige Intensität industriellen Produktdesigns. Und beim Museum der Universität von Alicante wählt Alfredo Payá einen stärker metaphysischen Ansatz, indem er physische Details zu einer Handvoll abstrakter metaphorischer Beziehungen kondensiert, eine Strategie, die an die Arbeit des Madrider Architekten und Lehrers Alberto Campo Baeza und die Kapellen von Tadao Ando erinnert.

Unter den wenigen jungen spanischen Architekten, die sich der mächtigen Strömung des neuen Minimalismus widersetzen, ist Alejandro Zaera mit seiner Architektur als Experiment einer wirklich globalen Praxis erwähnenswert. Zaera machte sich zuerst als Student durch seine Beiträge für die einflußreiche Zeitschrift *El Croquis* einen Namen, die in den frühen 80er

highly individual formal approach with an essentially global position, while maintaining important ties to Spain. It is interesting to compare this model of a trans-national practice with that of Rafael Moneo, who, although he works on projects across Europe and the United States, has never lost his moorings in an essentially Spanish frame of reference.

Federico Soriano and Dolores Palacios share with Zaera and Moussavi an inclusive approach to design, which borrows from other fields to broaden the range of architectural language. In the 1999 Euskalduna Opera in Bilbao, these borrowings range from a story-like metaphor that animates the basic design – the idea of the auditorium as an unfinished, rusty hull from the former shipyard on the site, sur-

Alfredo Payá
Alicante University Museum
Museum der Universität Alicante

Javier García-Solera
Business School,
University of Alicante
Wirtschaftsfakultät, Universität Alicante

rounded on three sides by foyers and services like construction scaffolding – to the actual construction of the auditorium shell by a local shipyard using naval structural techniques. The architects emphasize that they are not interested in the literal details of these sources, but rather in the formal object that results from their transposition. The metaphoric armature is a rare attempt to communicate to a popular audience without renouncing formal innovation.

Another potential generator of alternative design strategies is through the formation of regionally-based schools far from the gravitational pull of Madrid and Barcelona. This has not quite happened in Galicia, which shows promise with its new school in La Coruña, distinguished teachers such as Manuel Gallego and César Portela, and several emerging practices, but which still offers young architects too few opportunities to flourish. In addition to Irisarri and Piñera, whose interest in novel materials and design strategies is often driven by impossibly small working budgets, we should mention Alfonso Penela, born in 1952, author of the impressive Business School at the University of Pontevedra in Vigo (1992–1996), Pedro de Llano, Fernando Blanco, Guillermo Bertólez and Alfredo Freixedo.

Jahren von zwei Architekten der neuen Generation, Fernando Márquez und Richard Levene, gegründet wurde. Seine Studien in Harvard, wo Moneo Dekan war, und seine zweijährige Praktikumszeit im Rotterdamer Studio von Rem Koolhaas, erweiterten seinen Architekturhorizont. Gemeinsam mit seiner im Iran geborenen Frau Farshid Moussavi lehrt er heute als Professor an der Londoner Architectural Association. So kombi-

niert er wie Ricardo Bofill, Santiago Calatrava und Enric Miralles einen äußerst individuellen formalen Ansatz mit einer im wesentlichen globalen Position, wobei seine Beziehungen zu Spanien wichtig bleiben. Es ist interessant, sein Modell einer transnationalen Praxis mit Rafael Moneos Werk zu vergleichen, der seinen grundlegenden spanischen Bezugsrahmen nie verloren hat.

Federico Soriano und Dolores Palacios teilen mit Zaera und Moussavi einen umfassenden Gestaltungsansatz, der Anleihen in anderen Gebieten macht, um das Spektrum ihrer Architektursprache zu verbreitern. Bei der Euskalduna Oper in Bilbao von 1999 reichen diese Anleihen von einer narrativen Metapher, die die Grundgestaltung belebt – die Idee des Auditoriums als torsohafter rostiger Schiffsrumpf aus der ehemaligen Schiffswerft auf dem Grundstück, den an drei Seiten Foyers und Servicebereiche wie ein Baugerüst umgeben –, bis hin zur Ausführung dieses Gerüsts durch eine örtliche Werft, die dabei Techniken aus dem Schiffsbau einsetzte. Die Architekten betonen, daß sie nicht an wörtlichen Zitaten aus diesen Quellen interessiert sind, sondern an dem formalen Objekt, das aus ihrer Übertragung entsteht. Der metaphorische Anker ist ein seltener Versuch, mit dem breiten Publikum zu kommunizieren, ohne die formale Innovation preiszugeben.

Eine andere potentielle Quelle alternativer Entwurfsstrategien besteht in der Bildung regional verwurzelter Schulen weitab von den Gravitationszentren Madrid und Barcelona. Soweit ist es in Galicien noch nicht, wo es mit der neuen Schule in La Coruña, ausgezeichneten Lehrern wie Manuel Gallego und César Portela sowie mehreren neuen Architekturbüros

In the Canary Islands, the case for an alternate regional design culture is stronger. Its independent character was invigorated in the 1950s and 1960s by artist César Manrique's unique fusion of architecture and landscape on the volcanic island of Lanzarote. The intuitive, angular designs of Manuel Feo, Victor Alonso and Juan José Espino are the latest manifestation of the archipelago's more expressive tendencies, which include the rough, board-formed concrete compositions of the slightly more established studio of Artengo, Menis and Pastrana, in works such as the 1994 Proa Apartments in Santa Cruz de Tenerife and the Tenerife Parliament, currently under construction. María Luisa González, in contrast, born in 1953, has just completed her first major work, an office building for the regional government of Las Palmas, in a well-honed minimalist idiom.

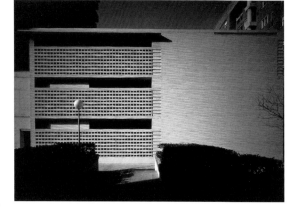

We should not close without mentioning other architects of interest among the new generation, whose work has appeared in Spanish publications and exhibitions over the past five years.[3] Madrid is particularly strong as a center for emerging practices, in part because its architects have found work in many parts of Spain. They include the studio of Pemjean, Martínez and Pemjean, authors of the 1996 Madarcos Town Hall outside Madrid, built in rubble stonework; Sol Madrilejos and Juan Carlos Sancho, authors of the 1996 Valvanera Gymnasium in San Sebastián de los Reyes, Madrid; Beatriz Matos and Alberto Martínez Castillo, winners of a special mention in the 1996 international competition to enlarge the Prado Museum; Samuel Torres and Pedro Palmero, authors of the 1998 University of Alicante Library, which has interesting similarities to the nearby buildings by García Solera and Payá; and Luis Rojo, who won the 1997 competition to build a theater and concert hall in Guadalajara (with Àngel Verdasco and Begoña Fernández-Shaw).

Other studios of note in Madrid are those of Sergio de Miguel, Eduardo Pesquera and Jesús Ularguia; María José Aranguren and José González Gallegos; Victoria Acebo and Ángel Alonso; Ricardo Sánchez Lampreave; and the Cano

zwar verheißungsvolle Ansätze gibt, junge Architekten jedoch zu geringe Entfaltungsmöglichkeiten erhalten. Neben Irisarri und Piñera, die ihr Interesse an neuen Materialien und Gestaltungsstrategien häufig mit absurd kleinen Budgets verwirklichen müssen, verdienen Pedro de Llano, Fernando Blanco, Guillermo Bertólez, Alfredo Freixedo und Alfonso Penela Erwähnung. Penela, geboren 1952, schuf die beeindruckende Wirtschaftsfakultät der Universität von Pontevedra in Vigo (1992–1996).

Auf den Kanarischen Inseln gibt es deutlichere Anzeichen einer alternativen regionalen Entwurfskultur. Ihr unabhängiger Charakter wurde in den 50er und 60er Jahren von der einzigartigen Verschmelzung von Architektur und Landschaft gestärkt, die der Künstler César Manrique auf der Vulkaninsel Lanzarote schuf. Die intuitiven, winkligen Entwürfe von Manuel Feo, Victor Alonso und Juan José Espino sind die jüngste Manifestation der expressiveren Tendenzen der Inselgruppe, zu denen die rauhen, Schalungsbetonkompositionen des schon etwas etablierteren Büros von Artengo, Menis und Pastrana bei Werken wie den Proa-Apartments von 1994 in Santa Cruz, Teneriffa, und dem Parlament von Teneriffa gehören, das gegenwärtig im Bau ist. María Luisa Ganzález, geboren 1953, hat im Kontrast dazu gerade ihr erstes großes Werk fertiggestellt, ein Bürogebäude für die Regionalregierung in Las Palmas, das eine gediegene minimalistische Formensprache kennzeichnet.

Wir sollten nicht schließen, ohne andere interessante Architekten der neuen Generation zu erwähnen, deren Arbeiten in spanischen Publikationen und Ausstellungen in den letzten fünf Jahren veröffentlicht wurden.[3] In Madrid gibt es besonders viele neue Architekturbüros, zum Teil deshalb, weil die Architekten der Stadt in vielen Regionen Spaniens Arbeit fanden. Dazu gehören das Büro von Pemjean, Martínez und Pemjean, die das 1996 in Bruchsteinmauerwerk ausgeführte Rathaus von Madarcos außerhalb von Madrid schufen; Sol Madrilejos und Juan Carlos Sancho, die 1996 die Valvanera-Sporthalle in San Sebastián de los Reyes, Madrid, bauten; Beatriz Matos und Alberto Martínez Castillo, die beim internationalen

De Miguel & Leache
Azpilagaña Medical Clinic, Pamplona
Azpilagaña-Klinik

Tabuenca & Leache
Frontón, Urroz-Villa
Frontón-Stadion

Pintos clan, Diego, Gonzálo, Alfonso and Lucia, three sons and a daughter of the late Madrid architect Julio Cano Lasso.

In Barcelona, the large and active generation of 1992 has not left many opportunities for its successors, and public building, though vigorous, has not returned to the grand scale of the Olympic preparations. The strong regional identity of Catalunya, backed by local cultural policies and institutions, has cost Barcelona architects the wider geographic base that their talents would seem to merit. Though generally better connected internationally than their Madrid peers, Barcelona architects are a weak presence in Madrid and many other parts of Spain. There are signs that some of the negative effects of Catalan isolation are being addressed, such as the recent upgrading of the prestigious FAD Awards (organized by Barcelona's *Foment de les Arts Decoratives*) from a local to a national event. But the current climate has allowed only a few new studios to emerge.

Irisarri & Piñera
Segade House, Fragosela
Haus Segade

Manuel Feo et al
Unelco Offices, San Bartolomé
de Tirajana
Unelco-Büros

In addition to the architects featured here, worth noting are the studio of Artigues, Castañeda, Heinrich, Roig and Tarrasó, authors of the 1996 Barceloneta harborfront park in Barcelona; Lluís Jubert and Engenia Santacana, whose first building, a small semi-buried house in Púbol, Girona, won the 1998 FAD Architecture Prize; Ton Salvadó and Esteve Aymerich, authors of a 1997 covered playing field in Vilafranca del Penedès, Barcelona, and a recent recycling plant in Girona; and Mercé Berengué and José M. Roldán, authors of a 1997 school in San Pere de Ribes, Barcelona.

The combination of a carefully-studied realism of limited means and a spartan nobility of spirit is encountered again and again in the work of the new generation. This dialectic is related both to the actual economic situation of Spain, and to issues present through much of its history. Its early form is religious, as seen in the 17th century still-life paintings of

Wettbewerb zur Erweiterung des Prados von 1996 lobend erwähnt wurden; Samuel Torres und Pedro Palmero, die 1998 die Bibliothek der Universität von Alicante schufen, welche interessante Ähnlichkeiten zu nahegelegenen Gebäuden von García Solera und Payá aufweist; sowie Luis Rojo, der 1997 den Wettbewerb für den Bau des Theaters und der Konzerthalle in Guadalajara gewann (zusammen mit Ángel Verdasco und Begoña Fernández-Shaw).

Andere bemerkenswerte Büros in Madrid sind Sergio de Miguel, Eduardo Pesquera und Jesús Ularguia; María José Aranguren und José González Gallegos; Victoria Acebo und Ángel Alonso; Ricardo Sánchez Lampreave; sowie die Familie Cano Pintos: Diego, Gonzalo, Alfonso und Lucia, die drei Söhne und eine Tochter des verstorbenen Architekten Julio Cano Lasso.

In Barcelona hat die große und aktive Generation von 1992 ihren Nachfolgern weniger umfangreiche Möglichkeiten übriggelassen, und die öffentliche Bautätigkeit hat, obwohl noch sehr rege, nicht mehr die Ausmaße der Olympia-Vorbereitungen. Die von der örtlichen Kulturpolitik und Kulturinstitutionen unterstützte stark regionale Identität Kataloniens hat die Architekten von Barcelona die breitere geographische Basis gekostet, die ihre Talente wohl verdient hätten. Obwohl sie im allgemeinen bessere internationale Kontakte haben als ihre Madrider Kollegen, sind die Architekten Barcelonas in Madrid und anderen Teilen Spaniens nur schwach vertreten. Es gibt Anzeichen, daß man etwas gegen einige der negativen Auswirkungen des katalanischen Isolationismus unternimmt, wie zum Beispiel die kürzliche Aufwertung des prestigeträchtigen FAD-Preises (den *Fomet de les Arts Decoratives* in Barcelona vergibt) von einem lokalen zu einem nationalen Preis. Aber im gegenwärtigen Klima konnten nur wenige Architekturbüros entstehen.

Neben den hier präsentierten Architekten verdienen die Studios von Artigues, Castañeda, Heinrich, Roig und Tarrasó Er-

Juan Sánchez Cotán and Zurburán, in which humble household objects, vegetables, fruit and game are depicted with a startling intensity, their earthy material presence and quiet lighting transmitting a suggestion of divine presence. Cervantes' Quixote and the allegorical paintings of Velázquez are secular, baroque variations on the theme, playing on the gulf between a base realism and the imagination.

The duality in these works can be related to the harsh contrasts of the landscape of central Spain, its oppressive light and deep interior shadows, the astonishing fruitfulness of its parched earth. It also has a historic dimension, in the exhaustion of the country's human and material resources and its backward economic development, which begins even before the decline of the empire and extends through Franco's 40-year regime.

In the architecture of the new generation, this duality is, I think, also a distant reflection of the 18th century Project of Reason, long frustrated and postponed in Spain but remem-

Juan Ignacio Mera
Subsidized Housing, Loranca,
Fuenlabrada
Gefördertes Wohnungsbau-
projekt

bered in the Marxist and leftist political tradition, and present in the minds of many as an unfulfilled ideal, given new life by Spain's political transition. In this strange but characteristic metamorphosis, a religious spirit is reborn, though transformed, in the secular movement that replaces it.

This is perhaps a roundabout way to account for the optimism and directness of Spain's new architecture. The fast

wähnung, die 1996 den Hafenpark Barceloneta in Barcelona schufen; Lluís Jubert und Engenia Santacana, deren erstes Gebäude, ein kleines, halb in der Erde versenktes Haus in Púbol, Girona, den FAD-Architekturpreis von 1998 gewann; Ton Salvadó und Esteve Aymerich, Schöpfer eines überdachten Spielfeldes in Vilafranca del Penedès in Barcelona von 1997 sowie einer kürzlich errichteten Abfallaufbereitungsanlage in Girona; sowie Mercé Berengué und José M. Roldán, die 1997 eine Schule in San Pere de Ribes, Barcelona, schufen.

Die Kombination eines sorgfältig ausgearbeiteten Realismus begrenzter Mittel und eines spartanischen Geistesadels findet sich immer wieder in den Werken dieser neuen Generation. Diese Dialektik hat sowohl etwas mit der wirtschaftlichen Situation Spaniens wie mit Themen zu tun, die in seiner ganzen Geschichte präsent sind. Ihre frühe Form ist religiös, wie man es in den Stilleben von Juan Sánchez Cotán und Zurburán aus dem 17. Jahrhundert sieht, bei denen einfache Haushaltsgegenstände, Gemüse, Obst und Wild mit verblüffender Intensität dargestellt werden, wobei ihre erdige materielle Präsenz und die ruhige Beleuchtung eine göttliche Gegenwart nahelegen. Cervantes' Don Quixote und die allegorischen Gemälde von Velázquez sind jahrhundertealte, barocke Variationen des Themas und spielen mit dem Abgrund zwischen einem niedrigen Realismus und der Vorstellungskraft.

Die Dualität dieser Werke kann auf die schroffen Kontraste der Landschaft Zentralspaniens bezogen werden, ihr unerbittliches Licht und ihre tiefen Schatten, die erstaunliche Fruchtbarkeit ihres ausgedörrten Bodens, und sie hat in der Erschöpfung der menschlichen und materiellen Ressourcen des Landes und der rückständigen wirtschaftlichen Entwicklung, die noch vor dem Niedergang des Reiches begann und durch die vierzigjährige Franco-Herrschaft hindurch andauerte, auch eine historische Dimension.

In der Architektur der neuen Generation ist diese Dualität, wie ich meine, auch ein entfernter Reflex der Aufklärung des 18. Jahrhunderts, die in Spanien lange Zeit nicht zum Zuge kam und aufgeschoben wurde, aber in der marxistischen und linken politischen Tradition bewahrt wurde und für viele als ein unerfülltes Ideal präsent geblieben ist. Spaniens politischer Wandel hat diesem Ideal neues Leben eingehaucht. In dieser seltsamen, aber charakteristischen Metamorphose wird der religiöse Geist, den die säkulare Bewegung abgelöst hat – wenn auch verwandelt – wiedergeboren.

Dies ist vielleicht eine etwas umständliche Erklärung für den Optimismus und die Direktheit der neuen spanischen Architekten. Die schnelle Geschwindigkeit der Entwicklung hat den Architekten wenig Zeit für philosophische Überlegungen gelassen. Die sich rasch wandelnde Landschaft, die rasche Errichtung von Spaniens erstem Autobahnnetz, von Flughäfen und Bürokomplexen, die Ausprägung einer Funktionstrennung amerikanischen Stils und der Bau von Einkaufsgalerien, die

pace of development hasn't allowed architects much time for philosophical reflection. The quickly changing landscape, the rapid construction of Spain's first complete network of divided highways, of airports and office parks, of American-style subdivisions and shopping malls, and the prosperous, happy new consumers who flock to use them (not to forget the proud colonies of subsidized housing, the gleaming public industrial parks, the high-tech mass transit systems), remind one of the euphoric postwar expansion of the American suburbs. The best young Spanish architects share this spirit. Every new public building they design, every library, school, sports center and housing project, has the bright freshness and uncomplicated promise of a new car or ranch house in the American 1950s. Old Spain has been made young again, full of confidence, technical know-how, and bright hope in a constantly improving future.

wohlhabende, glückliche neue Konsumenten bevölkern (ganz zu schweigen von den stolzen Kolonien öffentlich geförderter Wohnbauten, den leuchtenden Industrieparks, den High-Tech-Massentransportsystemen), erinnern an die euphorische Expansion amerikanischer Vorstädte nach dem Krieg. Die besten jungen spanischen Architekten teilen diesen Geist. Jedes neue öffentliche Gebäude, das sie entwerfen, jede Bibliothek, jede Schule, jedes Sportzentrum und Wohnhausprojekt hat die glänzende Frische und die unkomplizierte Verheißung eines neuen Autos oder eines neuen Landhauses im Amerika der 50er Jahre. Das alte Spanien ist wieder jung geworden, voller Selbstvertrauen, technischem Know-how und strahlender Hoffnung in eine sich beständig verbessernde Zukunft.

1 For books covering this period, see:

Richard Levene and Fernando Márquez, editors, *Arquitectura Española Contemporánea 1975/1990*, El Croquis Editorial, Madrid, 1989;

Muestra de 10 Años de Arquitectura Española 1980–1990, Ministerio de Obras Públicas y Transporte (MOPT), Consejo Superior de los Colegios de Arquitectos de España, Universidad de Menéndez-Pelayo, publishers, Madrid, 1991;

Pauline Saliga, Martha Thorne, editors, *Building in a New Spain: Contemporary Spanish Architecture*, The Art Institute of Chicago, Gustavo Gili, Barcelona, 1992.

2 The partners of Equipo Auia are Alfredo Villanueva, Manuel Paredes, Fernando Prats and Mario Muelas.

3 Good sources of compiled information on the new generation:

Catalogs for the Biennials of Spanish Architecture, especially editions III (1995), IV (1997) and V (1999), published in Madrid by the Ministerio de Fomento, the Consejo Superior de los Colegios de Arquitectos de España, and the Universidad de Menéndez-Pelayo of Santander;

Catalogs for the biannual *Muestra de Arquitectos Jóvenes*, II (1992), III (1994), IV (1996) and V (1998), published by the Fundación Camuñas, Madrid;

Annual *AV Monographs Yearbook* (Madrid), and annual year-end Spanish surveys of *El Croquis* (Madrid) since about 1995;

Architecti 15-16 (Lisbon), Sep-Nov 1992, issue dedicated to emerging Spanish firms;

Arquitectura Viva 46, Jan-Feb 1996, "Sangre fresca," issue dedicated to the new generation.

1 Vgl. zu dieser Periode die folgenden Publikationen: Richard Levene, Fernando Márquez (Hg.), *Arquitectura Española Contemporánea 1975/1990*, Madrid 1989; *Muestra de 10 Años de Arquitectura Española 1980–1990*, Ministerio de Obras Públicas y Transporte (MOPT), Consejo Superior de los Colegios de Arquitectos de España, Universidad de Menéndez-Pelayo (Hg.), Madrid 1991; Pauline Saliga, Martha Thorne (Hg.), *Building in a New Spain: Contemporary Spanish Architecture*, Barcelona 1992.

2 Die Partner der Gruppe Equipo Auia sind Alfredo Villanueva, Manuel Paredes, Fernando Prats und Mario Muelas.

3 Gute Informationsquellen über die neue Generation sind: die Kataloge der Biennalen spanischer Architektur, insbesondere die Ausgaben III (1995), IV (1997) und V (1999), veröffentlicht in Madrid vom Ministerio de Fomento, Consejo Superior de los Colegios de Arquitectos de España und der Universität Menéndez-Pelayo in Santander; die Kataloge für die zweijährige „Muestra de Arquitectos Jóvenes", II (1992), III (1994), IV (1996) und V (1998), veröffentlicht von der Fundación Camuñas, Madrid; *AV Monographs Yearbook* (Madrid) sowie der jeweils zum Jahresende erscheinende Spanienüberblick der Zeitschrift *El Croquis* (Madrid) ab etwa 1995; die Ausgabe von *Architecti 15–16* (Lissabon), September-November 1992, die sich mit neuen spanischen Architekturbüros befaßt; sowie die Ausgabe *Arquitectura Viva 46*, Januar-Februar 1996, „Sangre fresca", die sich der neuen Generation widmet.

Iñaki Ábalos & Juan Herreros Madrid

With a number of published monographs dedicated to their projects and theoretical writings, and with their participation in several international competitions and exhibitions, such as the 1995 Light Constructions show at New York's Museum of Modern Art, Ábalos and Herreros (A+H) have received a notable degree of international recognition. Their work introduces into current theoretical debate the idea of an architecture of pure technique, a concept distilled from the legacy of Alejandro de la Sota.

Their initial studies of Le Corbusier and the skyscraper convinced them that, in the early Modern Movement, "technique revealed to the most alert the mechanisms with which to imagine another paradigm." Applying this insight to their own practice, they established a few tactical positions, set out in the essay *A Fragile Skin* and elsewhere.

The first of these was the idea of design by catalog, through the critical selection of manufacturer's standard parts, an economy and distancing of design effort which they compare to the working method of Andy Warhol, and oppose to high tech's immersion in the production process. A+H also propose to break with the Modern concept of the facade as a product or reading of interior functions, and the "semiotic analogy," in which the building represents certain values or conceptual contents. Instead, they argue for the skin of the building as a surface of intensity, for an architecture of "sense, not significance," the "comprehension of architecture as a corporal language with technical roots and expression, almost anthropomorphic, a kind of animistic vision." In their latest projects, such as the Valdemingómez Waste Treatment Center, they speculate on the condition of public space, urbanism and landscape in contemporary society, drawing on the writings of Deleuze and Guattari, Habermas, Rorty and others. Their investigations focus on the concept of *Areas of Impunity*, title of their 1997 monograph, spaces in which the potential of the contemporary subject can find realization outside the bounds of dominating economic and social forces.

Das Architekturbüro Ábalos und Herreros (A & H) hat durch seine Teilnahme an mehreren internationalen Wettbewerben und an Ausstellungen wie der Präsentation „Light Constructions" im New Yorker Museum of Modern Art 1995 auch außerhalb Spaniens bereits beträchtliche Anerkennung gewonnen. Darüber hinaus sind eine Reihe von Publikationen erschienen, die sich den Entwürfen und theoretischen Schriften der Architekten widmen.

Ihre Arbeit bereichert die gegenwärtige theoretische Debatte um die Idee einer Architektur reiner Technik, ein Konzept, das auf das Erbe Alejandro de la Sotas zurückgeht. Durch ihre anfänglichen Studien über Le Corbusier und die Hochhausarchitektur gelangten sie zu der Überzeugung, daß in der frühen modernen Architektur „die Mechanismen, die ein anderes Paradigma vorstellbar machen, für den aufmerksamen Beobachter in der Technik offenbart werden". Ábalos und Herreros wandten diese Einsicht bei ihren eigenen Arbeiten an und entwickelten dafür einige taktische Positionen, die sie unter anderem in ihrem Essay *A Fragile Skin* darlegten.

Die erste dieser Positionen war die Idee einer Gestaltung „nach dem Katalog", das heißt der kritischen Auswahl von Standardelementen der Baustoffindustrie. Diese Sparsamkeit bei der Gestaltung und das Abrücken von einem energischen Formwillen vergleichen die Architekten mit der Methode Andy Warhols und setzten sie dem Ansatz von High-Tech entgegen, der sich ganz auf den Produktionsprozeß konzentriert.

A & H treten außerdem dafür ein, mit dem modernen Konzept der Fassade als einem Produkt oder einer Lektüre interner Funktionen zu brechen und auf die „semiotische Analogie" zu verzichten, wonach das Gebäude bestimmte Werte oder konzeptionelle Inhalte repräsentiert. Statt dessen sollte ihrer Meinung nach die Gebäudehaut eine „Oberfläche der Intensität" sein, Baukunst „Sinn, nicht Bedeutung" schaffen und „Architektur als körperliche Sprache mit technischen Wurzeln und einem technischen Ausdruck" verstanden werden, als „beinahe anthropomorph, eine Art animistischer Vision".

In ihren jüngsten Entwürfen wie der Abfallaufbereitungsanlage Valdemingómez setzen sie sich mit den Bedingungen des öffentlichen Raums, mit Themen der Stadtplanung und der Landschaft in der zeitgenössischen Gesellschaft auseinander, wobei sie auf Schriften von Deleuze und Guattari, Habermas, Rorty und anderen zurückgreifen. Ihre Untersuchungen konzentrieren sich dabei auf die Idee, „Bereiche der Unbelangbarkeit" zu schaffen – so der Titel ihrer Publikation von 1997 –, das heißt Räume, in denen sich Menschen außerhalb der Begrenzungen der herrschenden ökonomischen und sozialen Kräfte verwirklichen können.

Luis Gordillo House Villanueva de la Cañada (Madrid), 1994–1996
Haus Luis Gordillo

Garden facade
Gartenfassade

Three-quarter view
of garden front
Dreiviertelansicht
der Gartenfront

Built for the well-known Madrid painter Luis Gordillo, the house occupies a tree-covered site to the north of Madrid. The steel framing establishes a clear and open structural module. The exterior is clad in Robertson panels (also often used by De la Sota), silver-gray in color, with windows screened by pivoting and hinged wood louvers. The house is designed in section, with a double-height living area overlooked by a Corbusian gallery that opens to a large roof terrace. A second terrace crowns the structure, with views over the treetops to the nearby Guadarrama mountains and a distant Madrid. The steel structure and aluminum panels, unusual in a domestic project, were chosen for their economy and lightness.

The architects took care to assure effective insulation, and use domestic finishes of parquet flooring and gypsum board walls. The metal joists and concrete-filled metal pan ceilings are finished in white fireproof paint and exposed. The building is a masterly essay in Ábalos & Herreros' theoretical premises: the De la Sotian focus on an architecture of pure technique, further distanced through the method of design by catalog; and the interest in the skin of the building as a surface of fascination, reflective and ambiguous.

Das Haus wurde für den bekannten Madrider Maler Luis Gordillo erbaut und steht nördlich von Madrid auf einem baumbestandenen Grundstück. Der Stahlrahmen schafft ein klares und offenes konstruktives Modul. Außen ist das Gebäude, dessen Fenster mit drehbaren Lamellen-Holzladen ausgestattet sind, mit silbergrauen Robertson-Paneelen verkleidet (die auch De la Sota häufig einsetzte). Das Haus ist so entworfen, daß sein Querschnitt von außen erkennbar ist, mit einem Wohnbereich in doppelter Geschoßhöhe, auf den eine Galerie im Stile Le Corbusiers blickt, die sich zu einer großen Dachterrasse hin öffnet. Von der zweiten Terrasse, die das Gebäude krönt, bieten sich Ausblicke über die Baumwipfel zu den Bergen der nahen Sierra de Guadarrama und das ferne Madrid. Die Stahlkonstruktion und die Aluminiumpaneele – für ein Wohnhaus ungewöhnlich – wurden aus Preisgründen und wegen ihrer Leichtigkeit gewählt. Die Architekten sorgten für eine gute Wärmedämmung und benutzen übliche Wohnhauselemente wie Parkettfußböden und Rigips-Wände. Die Metallträger und betongefüllten Deckenplatten aus Metall sind mit feuerfester weißer Farbe gestrichen und offen sichtbar.

Das Gebäude illustriert meisterhaft die theoretischen Prämissen von Ábalos & Herreros: die Konzentration auf eine Architektur reiner Technik im Stil De la Sotas, die durch die „Gestaltung nach dem Katalog" noch entrückter wirkt; und das Interesse an der Gebäudehülle als faszinierender, reflektierender und mehrdeutiger Oberfläche.

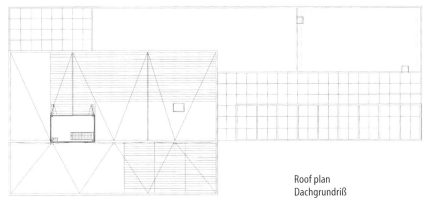

Roof plan
Dachgrundriß

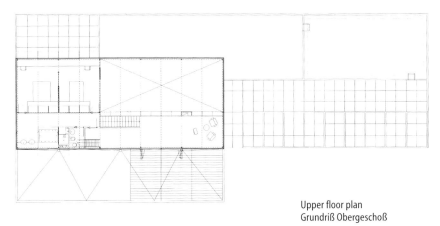

Upper floor plan
Grundriß Obergeschoß

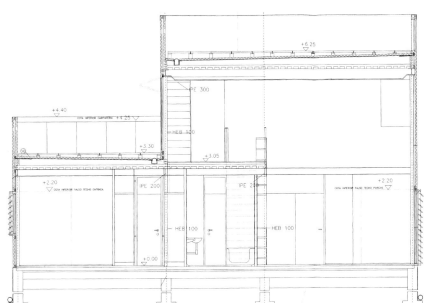

Living area,upper floor bath

Wohnbereich, Badezimmer im Obergeschoß

Section
Schnitt

Client
Auftraggeber
Luis Gordillo

Collaborators
Mitarbeiter
Rafael Hernández, Beatriz Inglés,
Javier Fresneda

Technical architect
Ausführungsplanung
Juan J. Núñez

Structural engineer
Tragwerk
Juan Gómez

Landscape architect
Landschaftsarchitektur
Fernando Valero

Builder
Generalunternehmer
Julio Morencos

Photos
Fotos
Angel Luis Baltanás &
Eduardo Sanchez,
Katsuida Kida

Usera Public Library   Madrid, 1995–96
Stadtbibliothek Usera

Right: 3rd floor
mezzanine plan
Left: 3rd floor plan

Rechts: Grundriß drittes
Halbgeschoß
Links: Grundriß drittes
Geschoß

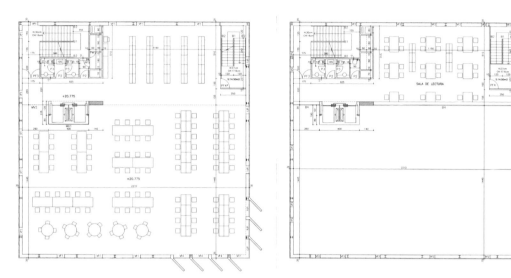

This competition-winning project, to be built in a southern suburb of Madrid, embodies the themes of the Gordillo House in a public setting. The library is arranged as a small tower above a broad buried plinth, a solution that frees a large part of the sloping site for a park, matches the scale of the adjacent municipal building, and captures views on the upper floors of the western horizon. The buried floor contains the lending collection, children's books and current periodicals. Its deep floor plate is naturally lit at the rear by a sunken patio, as well as by an intermediate clerestory that is expressed as a terrace-retaining wall on the exterior, taking advantage of the rising terrain. Succeeding floors are double-height and diaphanous, with rear mezzanine service areas. The first floor auditorium is followed by a second floor audio-visual center and the top floor reading room. The exteriors are clad in Robertson panels, with a light golden finish and slightly bowed surfaces to dramatically reflect the setting sun. The panels alternate haphazardly with floor-to-ceiling windows between the exposed floor slabs, and with projecting fins or blinders aimed at different views. Inside, A+H propose to finish the walls in wallpaper silkscreened with texts. Floors and ceilings are of exposed concrete, with the mix colored a slightly rosy hue.

Mit dem Entwurf dieser Stadtbücherei für einen südlichen Vorort von Madrid gewannen die Architekten den ausgeschriebenen Wettbewerb. Die Themen des Gordillo-Hauses sind hier in einem öffentlichen Gebäude umgesetzt. Die Bücherei ist als kleiner Turm über einem breiten unterirdischen Sockel konzipiert. Diese Lösung hält einen großen Teil des Hanggrundstücks für einen Park frei, entspricht den Dimensionen des angrenzenden Rathauses und bietet von den oberen Geschossen Ausblicke bis zum westlichen Horizont. Das unterirdische Geschoß enthält die Ausleihbibliothek, die Kinderbücher und die Zeitschriftenabteilung. Es wird am Ende durch einen abgesenkten Patio und – unter Ausnutzung des Terrains – einen als Terrassenstützmauer ausgebildeten Lichtgaden in der Mitte mit natürlichem Licht versorgt. Die oberen Geschosse mit Service-Bereichen auf einem Halbgeschoß haben doppelte Geschoßhöhe und sind sehr hell. Dem Auditorium des ersten Stocks folgt ein Audiovisionszentrum im zweiten und der Lesesaal im Obergeschoß.

Die Außenhaut besteht aus Robertson-Paneelen mit einem hellgoldenen Anstrich und leicht gekrümmten Flächen, in denen sich eindrucksvoll die untergehende Sonne spiegelt. Die Paneele wechseln sich ohne feste Ordnung mit raumhohen Fenstern zwischen den offen sichtbaren Deckenplatten sowie mit vorspringenden Finnen oder Scharten ab, die verschiedene Aussichten betonen. Innen wurden die Wände auf Vorschlag von A & H mit Tapeten verkleidet, die serigraphisch mit Texten bedruckt sind. Böden und Decken sind aus Sichtbeton mit einer leicht rosafarbenen Tönung.

Model
Modellansicht

Interior rendering
Innenansicht

Client
  Auftraggeber
Regional Government of Madrid

Collaborators
  Mitarbeiter
Angel Jaramillo, Miguel Kreisler,
Rocio Rein

Structural engineer
  Tragwerk
José M. Sierra

Mechanical engineers
  Haustechnik
José M. Cruz, Pedro J. Blanco

Model
  Modell
Jorge Queipo

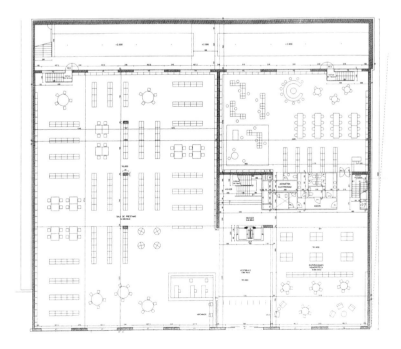

First floor plan
Grundriß erstes Geschoß

Model
Modellansicht

Site plan
Grundstücksplan

Section

Schnitt

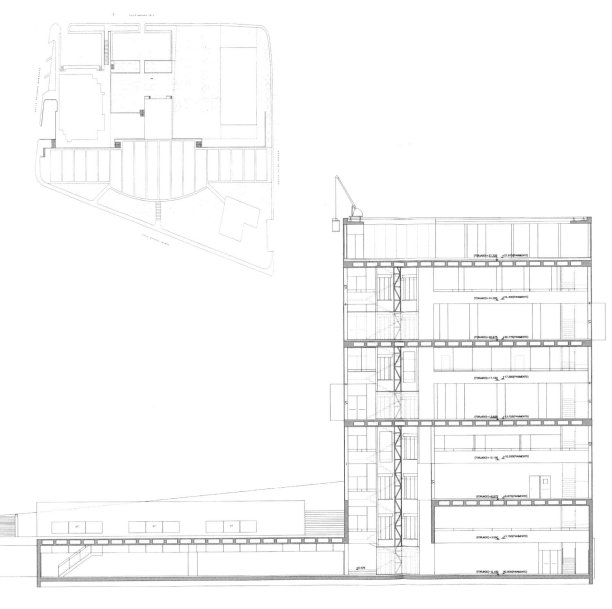

Valdemingómez Waste Treatment Center Madrid, 1997–
Abfallaufbereitungsanlage Valdemingómez

The architects have become specialists in landfills and waste treatment centers, sites which represent with particular intensity issues of the contemporary landscape. The existing landfill at Valdemingómez is to be stabilized and converted over 25 years into a public park, to be financed by the extraction and commercialization of its waste gases. An adjacent treatment facility serves the recycling of city garbage through a linear, gravity-fed classification mechanism. Its sloping roofs are covered with earth and planted to match the surrounding matorral; its exterior walls are translucent panels of recycled polycarbonate. The future park, which will be surrounded by densely-populated residential areas when finished, is an exercise in what the architects term an "area of impunity". It will support the same uses that undeveloped tracts of land outside any city are subject to: dirtbike circuits, horseback riding, roller-blading, glider flying, garden farming and the like, in an exploration of the peripheral wasteland as a new urban experience. The landscape design is a collage of organically-shaped spaces that follow the topography and cut and intersect with one another, forming open and enclosed areas, perspectival lines and other architectonic forms.

Die Architekten Ábalos und Herreros haben sich zu Spezialisten von Mülldeponien und Abfallaufbereitungsanlagen entwickelt, Orte, an denen Probleme der zeitgenössischen Landschaftsplanung besonders deutlich werden. Die vorhandene Mülldeponie in Valdemingómez soll stabilisiert und in den nächsten 25 Jahren nach und nach in einen öffentlichen Park verwandelt werden, der von der Gewinnung und Vermarktung von Abfallgasen finanziert werden soll. In einer angrenzenden Müllsortieranlage mit einem auf Schwerkraft beruhenden Sortiermechanismus wird der Hausmüll der Stadt zur Wiederaufbereitung getrennt. Ihre Schrägdächer sind passend zum umliegenden Dickicht mit Erde bedeckt und bepflanzt; ihre lichtdurchlässigen Außenwände bestehen aus wiederaufbereitetem Polycarbonat.

Der künftige Park, der von dichtbesiedelten Wohngebieten umgeben sein wird, ist ein Beispiel für das, was die Architekten „Bereiche der Unbelangbarkeit" nennen. Er wird die gleichen Nutzungsmöglichkeiten bieten wie jedes andere unbebaute Areal außerhalb der Stadt: Mountainbike-Fahren, Reiten, Inline-Skating, Hanggliding, Schrebergärten und ähnliches. Ödland an der städtischen Peripherie wird so als neuer urbaner Erlebnisraum erkundet. Die Landschaftsgestaltung ist eine Collage aus organisch geformten Räumen, die der Topographie folgen, sich überschneiden und kreuzen und offene und geschlossene Bereiche, perspektivische Fluchtlinien und andere architektonische Formen bilden.

Client
 Auftraggeber
Vertresa, City of Madrid

Project architect
 Projektarchitekt
Angel Jaramillo

Collaborators
 Mitarbeiter
Efréná García-Grinda, Angel Borrego, David Franco, Pablo Martínez

Structural engineers
 Tragwerk
OMA, Agustín Obiol & Luis Moya

Mechanical engineers
 Haustechnik
Tecnología y Equipamiento, S.A.

Landscape architect
 Landschaftsarchitekt
Fernando Valero

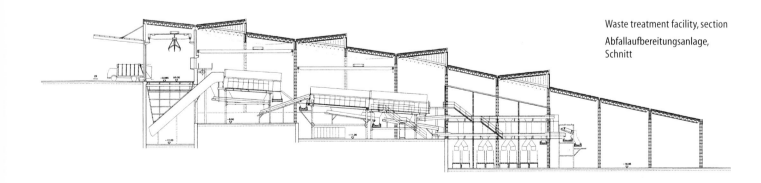

Waste treatment facility, section
Abfallaufbereitungsanlage, Schnitt

Waste treatment facility, model
Abfallaufbereitungsanlage,
Modellansicht

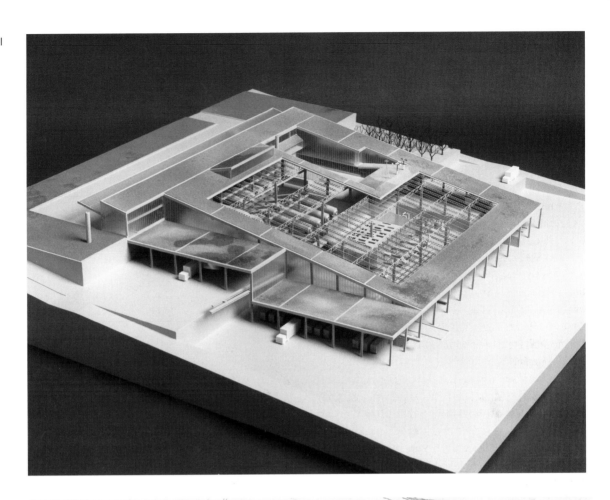

Landfill stabilization and land-
scape improvements, plan,
year 2011
Deponiestabilisierung und
Landschaftsverschönerung,
Plan bis 2011

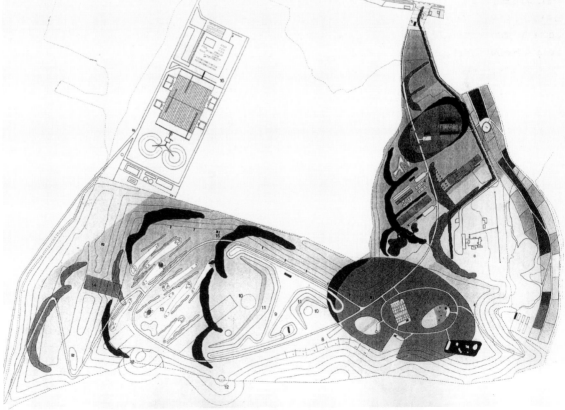

Mansilla + Tuñón Madrid

From their beginnings as top assistants to Rafael Moneo during the crucial years of 1983-1993, Luis Moreno Mansilla and Emilio Tuñón have gone on to become leaders of their generation. Active professors at the Madrid School of Architecture, editors of their own small press publication, *Circo*, and frequent participants in critical and theoretical endeavors, they have also won a stunning series of design competitions and awards, and maintain a busy, growing practice.

Mansilla and Tuñón exemplify the Spanish tradition of integrating theoretical and technical concerns in a single vision. Writing in *Circo 60*, they profess a formal restraint which recalls that of the late Spanish master Alejandro de la Sota: "Architecture isn't exactly silent. It is more like a conversation in lowered voices. Ideas are present, but the true effort lies in making them invisible."

A few characteristic formal traits have emerged in their work, which can be traced in part to Moneo's tectonic approach to design: the use of thick vertical wall sections, often with transparencies and translucencies, and often housing a zone of mechanical services, giving modern construction systems an added sense of depth and solidity; the parallel idea of a tectonic texture or weave as a representational gesture; a dense sectional choreography of space, from crenelated roof lines to dramatic interior sequences; and a corresponding condensation of the program into compact volumes, arranged in complex, subtle interaction with their context.

Seit ihren Anfängen als leitende Assistenten von Rafael Moneo in den entscheidenden Jahren zwischen 1983 und 1993 haben sich Luis Moreno Mansilla und Emilio Tuñón zu tonangebenden Vertretern ihrer Generation entwickelt. Sie unterrichten an der Madrider Architekturfakultät, geben ihre eigene kleine Publikation (*Circo*) heraus, beteiligen sich häufig an kritischen und theoretischen Debatten, haben daneben eine beeindruckende Zahl von Architekturwettbewerben und Preisen gewonnen und betreiben ein geschäftiges und wachsendes Büro.

Mansilla und Tuñón sind ein Beispiel für die spanische Tradition, theoretische und technische Aspekte zu einer einzigen Vision zusammenzuführen. In *Circo 60* bekennen sie sich zu einer formalen Zurückhaltung, die an den verstorbenen spanischen Meister Alejandro de la Sota erinnert: „Architektur ist durchaus nicht stumm, sie ist vielmehr wie ein Gespräch in gedämpftem Ton. Ideen sind gegenwärtig, aber die wahre Anstrengung liegt darin, sie unsichtbar zu machen."

Im Werk der Architekten tauchen einige charakteristische formale Züge auf, die sich teilweise auf Moneos tektonischen Gestaltungsansatz zurückführen lassen: Sie setzen dicke vertikale, oft mit transparenten und lichtdurchlässigen Elementen versehene Wände ein, hinter denen sich häufig die Haustechnik verbirgt. Damit verleihen sie modernen Konstruktionssystemen zusätzliche Tiefe und Solidität und betonen parallel dazu die Idee einer tektonischen Textur oder eines tektonischen Gefüges. Zu diesen formalen Merkmalen gehört ferner eine im Schnitt dichte Raumgliederung, vom zinnenartigen Dachabschluß bis zu Innenraumabfolgen von dramatischer Wirkung sowie eine entsprechende Verdichtung des Programms in kompakte Volumina, die in eine komplexe, subtile Interaktion mit ihrem Kontext treten.

Provincial Museum of Archeology and Fine Arts   Zamora, 1989–1996
Provinzmuseum für Archäologie und Kunst

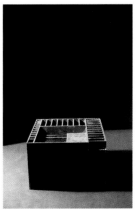

Gallery volume from upper city
Museumsbau von der Oberstadt

The Museum is located on the lower slopes of the ancient fortified hill town of Zamora, just outside the walls above the Duero River. The square-plan gallery volume is nestled behind surviving historic fragments, its sandstone walls blending with the retaining walls of the hill. Its visible facade is thus the roof, as seen from the upper city, with its emblematic grid of skylights/beams. The skylights are oriented according to the spanning directions of the galleries below, giving each a distinct character of light.

The entry is located at the back of the site. The circulation develops in the interstitial spaces between new and existing volumes, and between the galleries in the form of an enclosed central ramp. The thick walls lining the ramp house mechanical conduits, and are pierced by windows overlooking the galleries and niches for archeological epigraphs.

Das Museum liegt auf den unteren Hängen der alten befestigten Hügelstadt Zamora unmittelbar außerhalb der Stadtmauern oberhalb des Duero-Flusses. Der Baukörper mit quadratischem Grundriß, dessen Sandsteinwände mit der Farbe der Stützmauern des Hügels harmonieren, verbirgt sich hinter erhaltenen historischen Fragmenten. Seine einzige sichtbare Fassade ist somit das Dach mit seinem emblematischen Gitter von Dachverglasung und Trägern, wie man es von der Oberstadt aus sieht. Die Oberlichter orientieren sich an Ausrichtung und Abmessung der Ausstellungssäle unter ihnen und geben jedem einen eigenen Lichtcharakter.

Der Eingang liegt an der Rückseite des Grundstücks. Die Erschließung verläuft durch die Räume zwischen neuen und alten Volumina und, in Form einer umschlossenen zentralen Rampe, zwischen den Galerien. In den dicken Wänden entlang

Client
  Auftraggeber
Direction of State Museums,
Ministry of Culture

Technical architects
  Ausführungsplanung
Santiago Hernán,
J. Carlos Corona

Structural engineer
  Tragwerk
Alfonso G. de Gaite

Mechanical engineer
  Haustechnik
J.G. Associates

Builder
  Generalunternehmer
Fomento de Construcciones y
Contratas (FCC)

Chief of work
  Projektleiter
Enrique Pardo

Double-height Roman Gallery, with white concrete walls and teak floors

Römische Galerie in doppelter Geschoßhöhe mit weißen Betonwänden und Teakholzboden

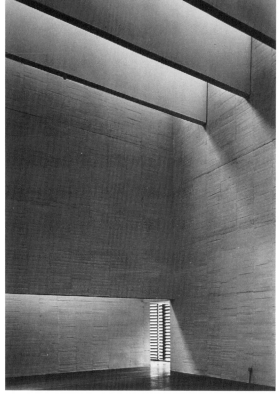

Central circulation ramp

Zentrale Erschließungsrampe

A restoration studio is separated from the gallery volume by a narrow sunken patio. The surrounding historic structures include parts of a 16th century palace, used for temporary exhibition galleries and offices, and the Santa Lucia Church, built in the 12th and 16th centuries and reconditioned for open collection storage.

der Rampe sind die Leitungssysteme der Haustechnik untergebracht. Sie haben Fensteröffnungen, durch die man auf die Ausstellungssäle und Nischen für die archäologischen Inschriften blicken kann. Eine Restaurationswerkstatt ist durch einen abgesenkten Patio vom Museum getrennt. Zu den umliegenden historischen Gebäuden gehören ein Schloß aus dem 16. Jahrhundert, in dem sich Säle für temporäre Ausstellungen befinden, und die Kirche Santa Lucia, die im 12. und 16. Jahrhundert erbaut wurde und zu einem offenen Magazin umgestaltet wurde.

East-west section: S. Lucia church to right; S. Cipriano in background

Ost-West-Schnitt: Rechts: Kirche Santa Lucia; Santo Cipriano im Hintergrund

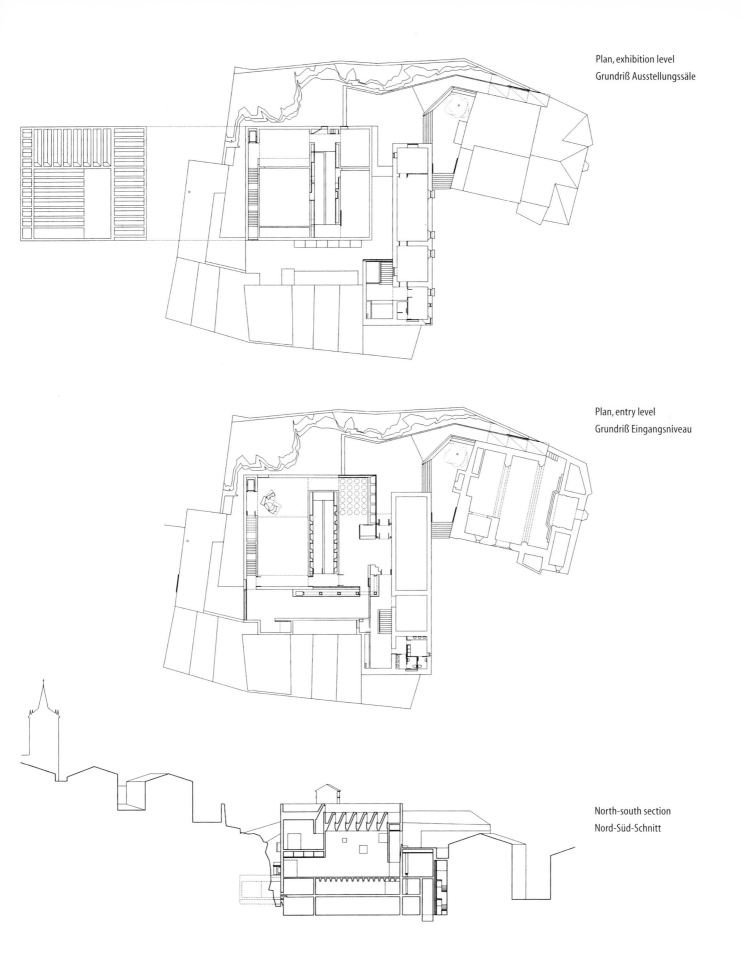

Plan, exhibition level
Grundriß Ausstellungssäle

Plan, entry level
Grundriß Eingangsniveau

North-south section
Nord-Süd-Schnitt

31

Castilla-León Concert Hall   León, 1995–
Castilla-León-Konzerthalle

Entry facade screening exhibition galleries (model)

Die Eingangsfassade schirmt die Ausstellungsflächen ab (Modell)

Study model from entry side

Studienmodell der Eingangsseite

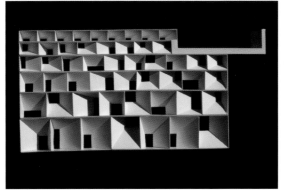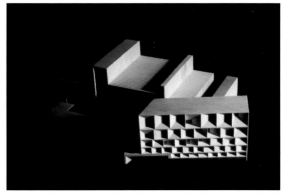

Client
  Auftraggeber
Junta of Castilla-León,
City of León

Technical architects
  Ausführungsplanung
Santiago Hernán, J. Carlos Corona

Structural engineer
  Tragwerk
Arup & Partners

Mechanical engineer
  Haustechnik
J.G. Associates

As in the Zamora museum, a disembodied facade engages a historic context. The concert hall volume is sheltered from the street by a low administrative block and a thick horizontal stone screen of irregular but mathematically-determined divisions, which incorporates the entry portico and exhibition galleries on its upper floor. The screen overlooks a plaza towards the Plateresque Hostal de San Marcos, on the western limits of the historic center.

The auditorium features two unequal seating areas facing each other on either side of the stage, following the model of J. M. García de Paredes' 1978 Manuel de Falla Concert Hall in Granada. It is a flexible space that can be configured for chamber music, orchestras, etc. and for a variable capacity of 600, 800 or 1200 spectators. Musicians access the stage via the lower level.

Mansilla + Tuñón have won the competition for the second phase of this regional cultural center, a museum which will be built behind the concert hall.

Wie beim Museum in Zamora stellt hier eine alte Fassadenwand den historischen Kontext her. Die Konzerthalle ist von der Straße durch einen niedrigen Verwaltungsblock und ein tiefes, horizontales Volumen aus Stein mit mathematisch bestimmten Unterteilungen abgeschirmt, in dem sich der Eingangsportikus und, im Obergeschoß, Ausstellungsflächen befinden. Dieses schützende Volumen überblickt die Plaza in Richtung des platresken Hostal de San Marcos am westlichen Rand des historischen Zentrums.

Das Auditorium verfügt über zwei ungleiche Sitzbereiche, die einander nach dem Modell von Garcías Manuel-de-Falla-Konzerthalle in Granada (1978) seitlich der Bühne gegenüberliegen. Es ist ein flexibler Raum, der für Kammermusik, Orchester etc. umgebaut und für eine wechselnde Kapazität von 600, 800 oder 1200 Sitzplätzen hergerichtet werden kann. Die Musiker gelangen über die untere Ebene auf die Bühne.

Mansilla & Tuñón gewannen auch den Wettbewerb für den zweiten Bauabschnitt dieses regionalen Kulturzentrums, ein Museum, das hinter der Konzerthalle gebaut wird.

Exploded axonometric

Explosionsaxonometrie

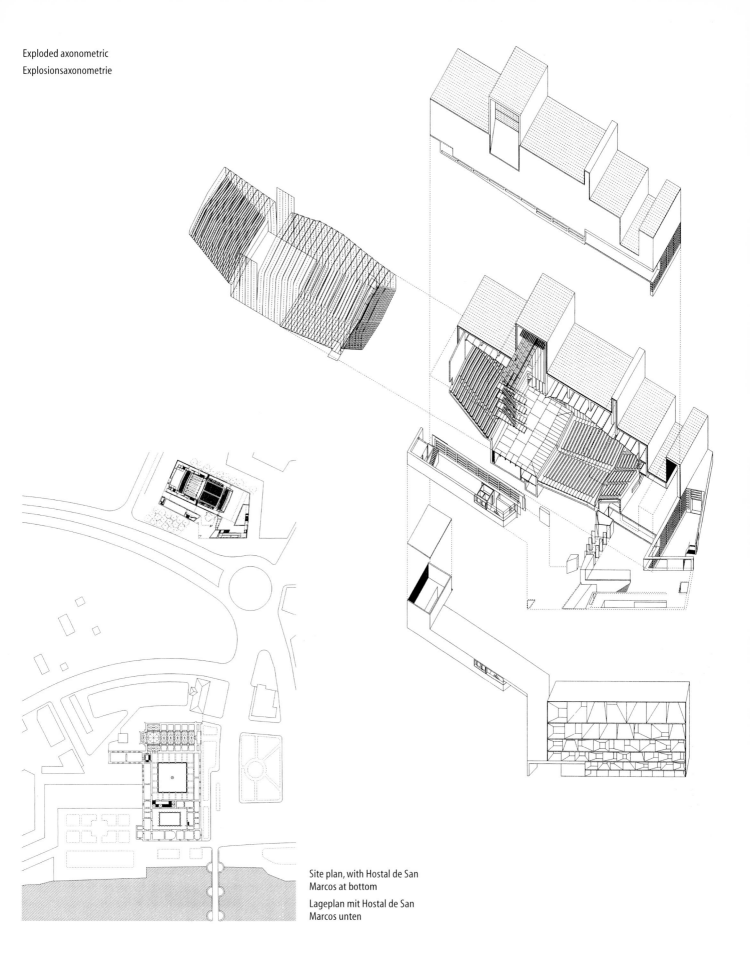

Site plan, with Hostal de San
Marcos at bottom

Lageplan mit Hostal de San
Marcos unten

Indoor Swimming Pool   San Fernando de Henares (Madrid), 1994–1998
Hallenbad San Fernando de Henares

A glass curtain wall within a basket of concrete louvers encloses the pools.

Innenansicht: Eine Glasfassade in einer Hülle aus Betonblenden umschließt die Schwimmbecken.

Client
  Auftraggeber
City of San Fernando de Henares

Technical architects
  Ausführungsplanung
Santiago Hernán, J. Carlos Corona

Structural engineer
  Tragwerk
Alfonso G. de Gaite

Mechanical engineer
  Haustechnik
J.G. Associates

Builder
  Generalunternehmer
FCC

This simple rectangular volume, added to existing recreational facilities, is composed of a glass enclosure surrounded by a basket weave of precast concrete louver elements. Its structure consists of precast concrete columns, beams and light planks. The pool level is elevated above a mechanical service zone, due to the high water line of its riverside site. Lockers are naturally lit by rows of skylit trenches. The gray tile of the pool deck has the effect of dematerializing the water plane, while the louvered walls splatter the space with bits of sunlight, and convert the structure into an illuminated jack-o'-lantern at night.

Dieser einfache rechteckige Baukörper, der den vorhandenen Freizeiteinrichtungen hinzugefügt wurde, besteht aus einer Glashülle, die von einer korbgeflechtartigen Blendwand aus vorgefertigten Betonlamellen umgeben ist. Die Konstruktion besteht aus vorgefertigten Betonstützen, Trägern und leichten Bohlen. Das Schwimmbecken ist aufgrund des hohen Wasserspiegels des Flußgrundstücks angehoben, so daß darunter Raum für technische Installationen entstand. Die Umkleidekabinen werden durch Reihen von Einschnitten mit natürlichem Licht erhellt. Die grauen Kacheln um das Becken haben den Effekt, die Wasserfläche zu entmaterialisieren, während die Lamellenwände Sonnenkleckse über den Raum verstreuen und das Gebäude bei Nacht in ein flackerndes Irrlicht zu verwandeln scheinen.

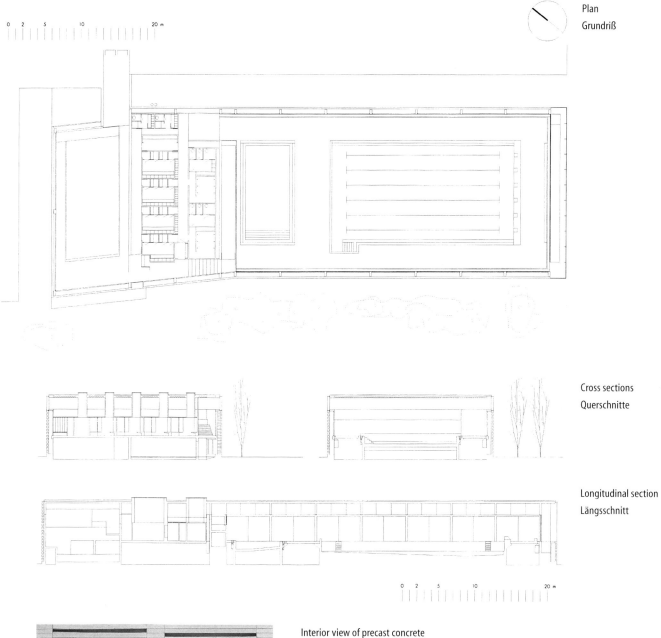

0 2   5   10   20 m

Cross sections

Querschnitte

Longitudinal section

Längsschnitt

0   2   5   10   20 m

Interior view of precast concrete
louver wall

Innenansicht der Blendwand aus
vorgefertigten Betonteilen

Museum of Fine Arts   Castellón, 1997–
Kunstmuseum

Client
  Auftraggeber
Castellón Cultural S.L.

Technical architects
  Ausführungsplanung
Santiago Hernán, J. Carlos Corona

Structural engineer
  Tragwerk
Alfonso G. de Gaite

Mechanical engineer
  Haustechnik
J.G. Associates

Builder
  Generalunternehmer
FCC

A dramatic diagonal cascade of double-height spaces visually links the five levels of galleries, drawing visitors from floor to floor. The crenelated profile of roof lights reappears from the architects' winning competition design for the El Aguila Cultural Center in Madrid.

The gallery volume and a new building for restoration studios frame the surviving cloister and chapel of a 1930s school, which are dedicated to administration areas. Interior finishes are similar to the Zamora museum, with hollow walls for mechanical distribution. The exterior is finished in panels of recycled aluminum, which are stamped along their borders with the Museum's name.

Eine dramatisch wirkende diagonale Kaskade von Räumen in doppelter Geschoßhöhe verbindet die fünf Ausstellungsgeschosse visuell und zieht den Besucher von Stockwerk zu Stockwerk. Die zinnenartige Silhouette der Oberlichter ist dem Entwurf der Architekten für das Kulturzentrum El Aquila Cultural in Madrid entnommen, mit dem sie den Wettbewerb gewannen.

Der Museumsbau und ein neues Gebäude mit Restaurationswerkstätten rahmen den erhaltenen Wandelgang mit Kapelle einer Schule aus den 30er Jahren, wo die Verwaltung untergebracht ist. Die Innenwände sind ähnlich wie beim Museum in Zamora behandelt, und ebenso wie dort sind die technischen Installationen in hohlen Wänden versteckt. Außen ist das Gebäude mit Paneelen aus wiederverwertetem Aluminium verkleidet, in deren Ränder der Name des Museums eingeprägt ist.

Model
Modellansicht

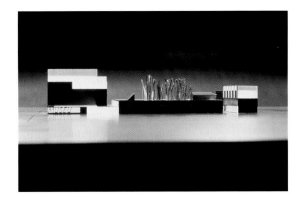

Section
Schnitt

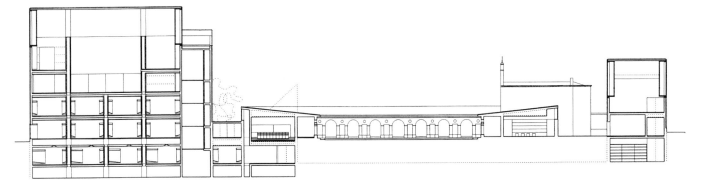

36

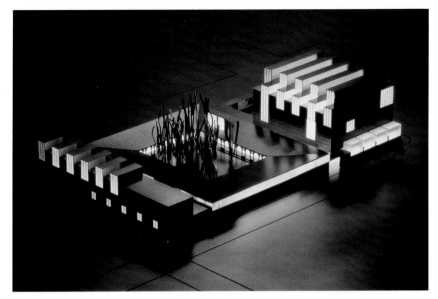

Model showing (l to r) restoration studios, administrative cloister, gallery volume

Modell mit (von links nach rechts): Restaurationswerkstätten, Verwaltungstrakt, Ausstellungsbereich

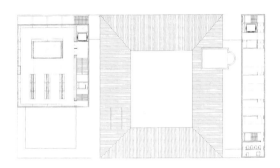

First floor plan

Grundriß Obergeschoß

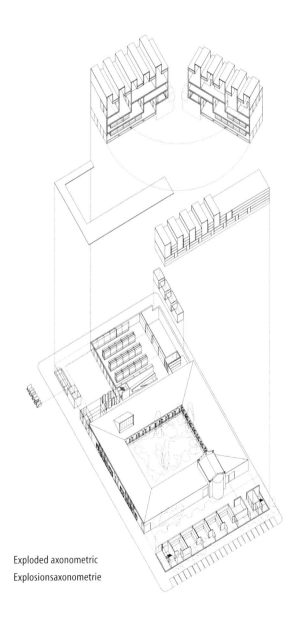

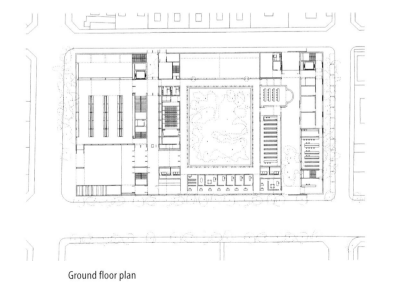

Ground floor plan

Grundriß Erdgeschoß

Exploded axonometric

Explosionsaxonometrie

María Fraile & Javier Revillo Madrid

Fraile and Revillo made their debut with the most uncompromising minimal work of their generation, the award-winning Zamora Trade Fair Pavilion. Their visceral rejection of post modern figuration, nurtured in part during their apprenticeships with Rafael Moneo, has led them to imagine a radically opposite formal aim. According to the architects, the Zamora design seeks no less than to "annul singularity, in so far as it is possible, and the figuration of architectural elements, to dilute and neutralize them in favor of the general space."

They place their work in continuity with the modern tradition, although they assume the post-modern relativization of Modernist abstraction. To the Miesian dictum "God is in the details," Revillo observes that the details more often reveal the hand of the builder, and the technical means at his disposal, fixing the work to a particular time and place. And Fraile emphasizes the need to introduce humanizing values to the raw technological logic of industrial building systems, through the choreography of spatial relationships, proportions, repetitions, the treatment of light and surfaces, and the choice of intimate details: in short, all the basic tools of the architect's craft.

The architects' subsequent designs are essentially variations on the themes introduced in Zamora, adapted to different programs and sites, and subject to different permutations. This development from project to project creates a conversation between the works, in which the latter designs reveal latent dimensions of the originating idea.

Fraile und Revillo debütierten mit dem kompromißlosesten und minimalistischsten Werk ihrer Generation, dem Messepavillon von Zamora, der den Wettbewerb gewann. Ihre instinktive Ablehnung postmoderner Formgebung, die sich zum Teil ihrer Lehrzeit bei Rafael Moneo verdankt, führte sie zur Konzeption eines radikal entgegengesetzten formalen Ziels. Den Architekten zufolge versucht der Zamora-Entwurf nichts Geringeres als „Einzigartigkeit und die Formgebung architektonischer Elemente, so weit dies möglich ist, aufzuheben, sie zugunsten des allgemeinen Raums abzuschwächen und zu neutralisieren".

Sie stellen ihre Arbeit in die Kontinuität der modernen Tradition, obwohl sie der postmodernen Relativierung der modernistischen Abstraktion folgen. Dem Diktum Mies van der Rohes, Gott stecke im Detail, entgegnet Revillo, daß die Details weit häufiger die Hand des Erbauers und die technischen Mittel offenbaren, die ihm zur Verfügung standen, und somit das Werk an eine bestimmte Zeit und einen bestimmten Ort binden. Und Fraile betont die Notwendigkeit, in die Zweckrationalität industriellen Bauens durch die Choreographie räumlicher Beziehungen, Proportionen, Wiederholungen, die Behandlung von Licht und Flächen und die Wahl vertrauter Details, kurz, durch alle dem Architekten zur Verfügung stehenden Werkzeuge humanisierende Werte einzuführen.

Die späteren Entwürfe der Architekten sind im wesentlichen Variationen der Themen, die sie in Zamora einführten, angepaßt an die verschiedenen Programme und Orte und auf unterschiedliche Weise abgewandelt. Diese Entwicklung von Werk zu Werk schafft einen Dialog zwischen ihren Arbeiten, in dem die späteren Entwürfe unterschwellig Dimensionen der ursprünglichen Idee offenbaren.

Trade Fair Exhibition Hall   Zamora, 1993–1996
Messehalle

Collaborators
  Mitarbeiter
Silvia de Anna, Francisco Rojo

Technical Architect
  Ausführungsplanung
Alfredo Blanco Pérez

Structural engineer
  Tragwerk
Luis Lasic Regina

Mechanical engineer
  Haustechnik
J.G. & Associates

Photos
  Fotos
Luis Asin, Francisco Rojo

Exhibition foyer
Ausstellungsfoyer

The building stands on the floodplain of the Duero River east of the city center, in an area dedicated to agricultural uses. The architects sought to "present the contained space of the structure like a fragment extracted from its surroundings, a circumstantial appropriation of the air," a premise they pursued using "notions of agricultural space: numbers, measures, geometry and repetition."

The square, 11,000 m^2 volume is raised on a concrete plinth for protection from occasional floods. A large foyer, suitable for receptions and freestanding displays, is separated from the main exhibit hall by a mezzanine containing the cafeteria, offices and services. The mechanical plant is contained in a small independent volume.

The foyer is enclosed in translucent glass panels, with a band of clear glass at the floor level that relates the rhythmic

Das Gebäude steht im Überschwemmungsgebiet des Duero östlich des Stadtzentrums in einem Gebiet, das landwirtschaftlich genutzt wird. Die Architekten versuchten, „den umschlossenen Raum des Gebäudes wie ein Fragment zu präsentieren, das aus seiner Umgebung extrahiert wurde, eine umfassende Inbesitznahme der Luft". Um dieses Ziel zu erreichen, setzten sie „Begriffe des landwirtschaftlichen Raumes ein: Zahlen, Maße, Geometrie und Wiederholung".

Der quadratische, 11.000 m^2 große Bau sitzt auf einem Betonsockel, der vor den gelegentlichen Überschwemmungen schützt. Ein großes Foyer, das sich für Empfänge und Ausstellungstafeln eignet, ist von der Hauptausstellungshalle durch ein Halbgeschoß getrennt, in dem sich die Cafeteria, Büros und Service-Einrichtungen befinden. Die Haustechnik ist in einem unabhängigen kleinen Gebäude untergebracht.

structural divisions of the space to the adjoining fields. The exhibit hall, designed for mounting display stands, is enclosed in corrugated metal panels and naturally lit by rows of continuous skylights. The rigorously modulated steel structure is fully exposed. On the facades, the two cladding systems are simply and roughly juxtaposed.

As in the work of Mies, the elevated plinth and high, handsome proportions confer an aura of grandeur on the human figures that occupy the building, an effect only heightened by its contrast with the tough tactile vitality of the concrete floor and thin industrial enclosure.

Das Foyer ist von lichtdurchlässigen Glaspaneelen umschlossen, wobei auf dem Niveau des Erdgeschosses ein Band von Klarglas die rhythmische Untergliederung des Raumes zu den angrenzenden Feldern in Beziehung setzt. Der Ausstellungssaal, der für Ausstellungsstände ausgelegt ist, ist von gewellten Metallpaneelen umgeben und wird durch Reihen durchlaufender Oberlichter natürlich belichtet. Die streng modulierte Stahlkonstruktion ist vollständig entblößt. An den Fassaden sind die beiden Verkleidungssysteme einfach und unvermittelt nebeneinandergesetzt.

Wie bei den Arbeiten von Mies van der Rohe verleihen der erhöhte Sockel und die schönen Proportionen den Menschen, die das Gebäude bevölkern, eine Aura der Erhabenheit, eine Wirkung, die vom Kontrast zur harten, fühlbaren Vitalität des Betonbodens und der dünnen industriellen Hülle nur noch gesteigert wird.

Location plan
Umgebungsplan

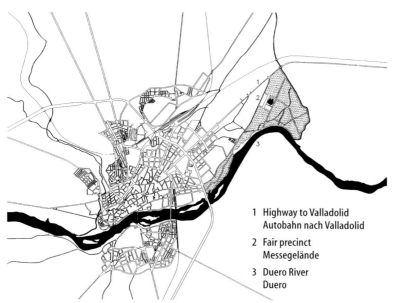

1 Highway to Valladolid
  Autobahn nach Valladolid

2 Fair precinct
  Messegelände

3 Duero River
  Duero

40

Mezzanine plan:
cafeteria, offices and services

Grundriß Halbgeschoß:
Cafeteria, Büros und Service-
Bereiche

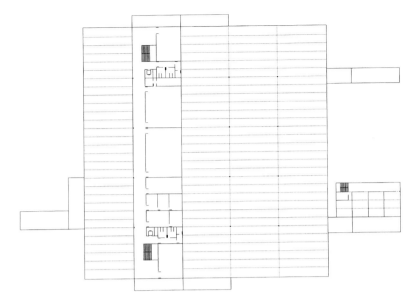

Ground level plan
Grundriß Erdgeschoß

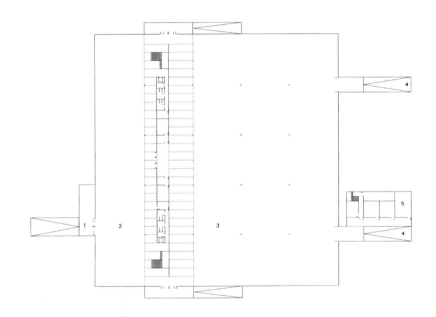

1 Main entry
  Haupteingang
2 Exhibition foyer
  Ausstellungsfoyer
3 Main exhibition hall
  Hauptausstellungshalle
4 Cargo entry
  Liefereingang
5 Mechanical services
  Haustechnik

Site plan
Lageplan

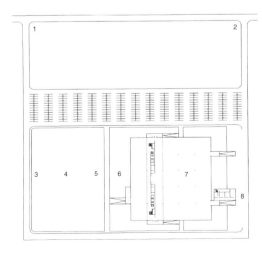

1 Visitors' entry
  Besuchereingang
2 Cargo entry
  Liefereingang
3 Service road
  Lieferzufahrt
4 Garden (future expansion)
  Garten (künftige Erweiterung)
5 Main entry
  Haupteingang
6 Exhibition foyer
  Ausstellungsfoyer
7 Main exhibition hall
  Hauptausstellungshalle
8 Mechanical services
  Haustechnik

Sports Center   Valdemoro (Madrid), 1992–1998
Sportzentrum

Interior, pool
Innenansicht Schwimmbad

Exterior detail
Detail der Außenfassade

Client
  Auftraggeber
Sports Division, Department of
Education and Culture, Regional
Government of Madrid; Munici-
pality of Valdemoro

Collaborators
  Mitarbeiter
Luis Díaz Mauriño, Francisco Rojo

Technical architects
  Ausführungsplanung
Santiago Hernán,
Juan Carlos Corona

Structural engineer
  Tragwerk
Florentino Moretín

Mechanical engineer
  Haustechnik
J.G. & Associates

Builders
  Generalunternehmer
1st phase, LAIM
2nd phase, ACS

Chief of work, 2nd phase
  Projektleiter, 2. BA
Antonio Aldeanueva

Photos
  Fotos
Francisco Rojo, David Cohn

In this recreational facility for a small town 24 kilometers south of Madrid, the inward focus of the spaces around themes of rhythm, proportion, light, and contained space intensifies. The building's Miesian, shed-like volumes are partially sunk into the sloping site, so that the entry offers direct access to spectator seating on the upper level. The two volumes of the pool and gym are separated on the upper level by a narrow exterior patio. Lower level dressing rooms, located under the spectator seating, receive light from this patio and from the translucent glass walls that separate them from the gym and pool.

The pool volume is clad in translucent sheets of glass above a concrete base, while only the north and south walls of the gym are translucent. The principal material for interior partitions and exterior cladding is galvanized steel sheet with a corrugated profile. The only clear glass offers a privileged viewpoint from the upper vestibule over the pool, with its roof trusses at eye level, and into the exterior patio, the only exterior view.

Bei dieser Freizeiteinrichtung für eine Kleinstadt 24 Kilometer südlich von Madrid sind die Räume mit Themen wie Rhythmus, Proportion, Licht und umschlossener Raum noch stärker nach innen ausgerichtet. Die „miesischen", hallenartigen Volumina des Komplexes sind teilweise in das Terrain des abschüssigen Grundstücks versenkt, so daß der Eingang direkten Zugang zu den Zuschauersitzen im Obergeschoß bietet. Die beiden Körper des Schwimmbads und der Turnhalle sind auf dem oberen Niveau durch einen schmalen äußeren Hof getrennt. Die Umkleideräume des unteren Niveaus, die unter den Zuschauersitzen liegen, erhalten ihr Licht vom Hof und durch lichtdurchlässige Glaswände, die sie von der Turnhalle und dem Schwimmbad trennen.

Die Schwimmhalle ist mit Glasscheiben über einem Betonsockel verkleidet, während bei der Turnhalle nur die Nord- und Südwände lichtdurchlässig sind. Das hauptsächliche Material für die inneren Trennwände und die Außenverkleidung sind verzinkte Stahlpaneele mit gewelltem Profil. Die einzige Klarglasfläche bietet vom oberen Foyer aus, mit den Dachträgern in Augenhöhe, eine gute Aussicht auf das Schwimmbecken und auf den Hof – der einzige Ausblick nach draußen.

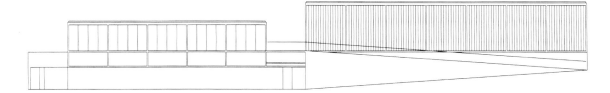

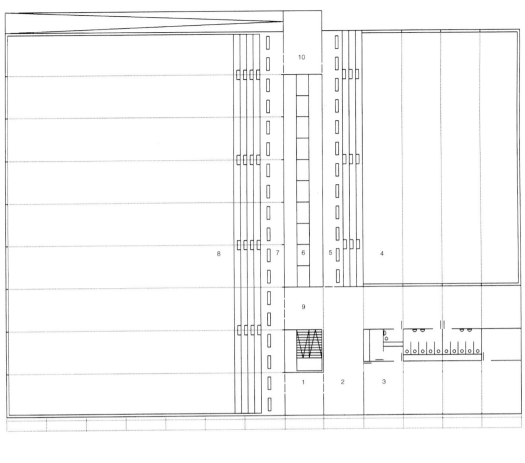

Upper entry level
Oberes Eingangsniveau

1 Public entry
   Öffentlicher Eingang
2 Lobby
   Lobby
3 Offices
   Büros
4 Pool below
   Schwimmbecken
5 Spectator seating
   Zuschauersitze
6 Exterior patio
   Außenhof
7 Spectator seating
   Zuschauersitze
8 Gym below
   Sporthalle
9 Stair to below
   Treppe nach unten
10 Emergency exit
   Notausgang

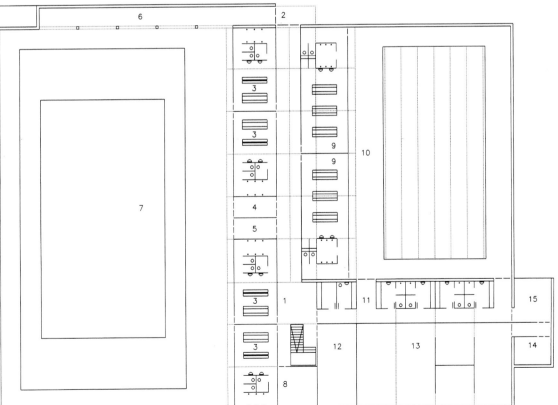

Lower court and pool level
Unterer Hof und Niveau des
Schwimmbeckens

1 Corridor
   Korridor
2 Exit to exterior playing court
   Ausgang zum Spielfeld vor
   dem Gebäude
3 Gym dressing rooms
   Umkleidekabinen Sporthalle
4 To gym
5 Zur Sporthalle
6 Storage
   Lagerraum
7 Gym
   Sporthalle
8 Maintenance
   Wartungsraum
9 Dressing rooms, pool
   Umkleidekabinen
   Schwimmbad
10 Pool
   Schwimmbecken
11 Staff dressing rooms
   Umkleideräume des
   Personals
12 Warm-up gym
   Aufwärmbereich
13 Mechanical
   Haustechnik
14 Boiler room
   Kesselraum
15 Access, maintenance
   Zugang Wartungsbereich

Berrrocal Museum   Algaidas (Málaga), 1997–
Berrocal Museum

Client
  Auftraggeber
Algaidas Foundation

Collaborators
  Mitarbeiter
Luca Donadoni, Francisco Rojo

The Museum and sculpture garden, run by a local public-private foundation, will house a collection of sculptures and drawings by Miguel Berrocal, a native-born artist who lives in Switzerland. The Museum is located on the eastern edge of the town, on a slope overlooking a *vaguada* or stream bed.

The division of the building into three equal parts, each 9 meters wide, produces two high halls separated by a middle zone of small galleries and patios. The Berrocal Gallery for the permanent collection, 9 meters high and 40 meters long, overlooks the vaguada and sculpture garden below through a horizontal glass slit at floor level. The second hall can be used for temporary exhibits, lectures and other events. Between them, the zipper-like alternation of patios and low gallery-niches, beginning with the entry and ending with the drawing gallery, admits natural light reflected from the marble surfaces of the patio walls and floors.

In conceptual terms, this mid-section slips below the main level with the slope of the site, producing a lower mezzanine for offices and library, and a ground level storage space. The mezzanine overlooks the garden through a loggia situated under the Berrocal Gallery. It is accessed from a service entrance on the building's northern elevation.

Das Museum und der Skulpturengarten, die von einer örtlichen öffentlich-privaten Stiftung getragen werden, werden eine Sammlung von Skulpturen und Gemälden von Miguel Berrocal beherbergen, einem im Ort geborenen Künstler, der heute in der Schweiz lebt. Das Museum liegt am Ostrand der Stadt an einem Hang, der eine *vaguada,* ein trockenes Flußbett überblickt.

Die Unterteilung des Gebäudes in drei gleiche Teile (jeder 9 Meter breit) schafft zwei hohe Hallen, die von einem mittleren Bereich mit kleinen Ausstellungsräumen und Innenhöfen getrennt sind. Die Berrocal-Galerie für die Dauerausstellung ist 9 Meter hoch und 40 Meter lang. Sie überblickt durch einen horizontalen Glasschlitz entlang des Fußbodens den darunterliegenden Skulpturengarten und die *vaguada*. Der zweite Saal kann für temporäre Ausstellungen, Lesungen und andere Veranstaltungen genutzt werden. Zwischen ihnen läßt der ineinandergreifende Wechsel von Höfen und niedrigen, nischenartigen Ausstellungsflächen, der mit dem Eingang einsetzt und bei dem Ausstellungsbereich für Zeichnungen endet, natürliches Licht ein, das von den Marmorflächen der Hofwände und -böden reflektiert wird.

Dieser mittlere Gebäudeteil ist so konzipiert, daß er sich aufgrund der Abschüssigkeit des Grundstücks unter das Hauptniveau schiebt und ein niedrigeres Halbgeschoß für Büros, eine Bibliothek sowie eine Abstellfläche auf dem Niveau des Erdgeschosses schafft. Das Halbgeschoß überblickt den Garten über eine Loggia, die unter der Berracal-Galerie liegt. Man erreicht sie über einen Nebeneingang an der Nordseite des Gebäudes.

Interior perspective
Perspektivische Innenansicht

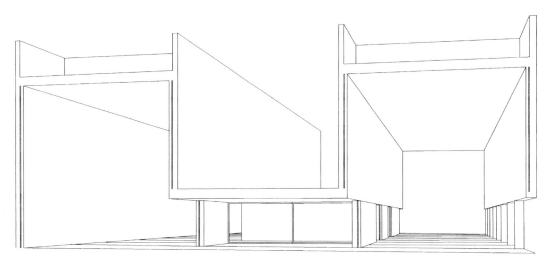

44

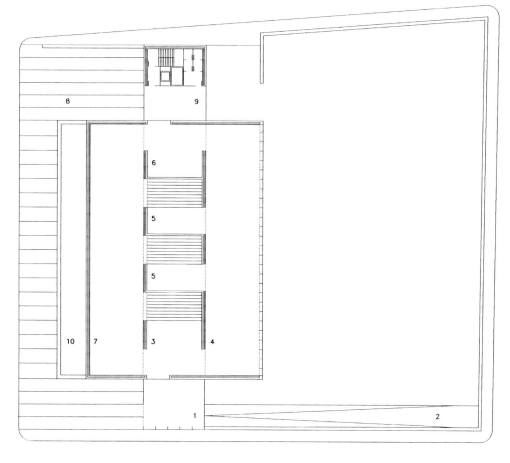

1 Public entry
Öffentlicher Eingang

2 Ramp down to garden
Rampe zum Garten hinunter

3 Foyer
Foyer

4 Berrocal Gallery
Berrocal-Galerie

5 Patio-galleries
Hofgalerien

6 Graphic works gallery
Graphik-Ausstellungsbereich

7 Temporary exhibitions, multi-use
Saal für temporäre Ausstellungen,
Vielzweckraum

8 Service access
Service-Zugang

9 Staff entry
Personaleingang

10 Patio
Hof

Juan Ignacio Mera   Madrid

While much of Spain's architectural debate rarely extends beyond the limited circle of the profession, and the "conversation in hushed voices" that Mansilla + Tuñón refer to, Juan Ignacio Mera finds himself in the tough outside world of commercial building, where he applies the rigorous principles of his Madrid School training in a daily struggle to win over clients, builders, and the public.

Mera maintains a staff of over 12 professionals, and a large portfolio in subsidized and commercial housing, as well as commercial buildings and public facilities, working as sole author or in collaborations. He confesses that he tries to avoid aesthetic discussions with his clients, but his high standards have served them well, contributing, for example, to the merit-based winning bids for public building sites by non-profit housing associations in Pamplona, Cáceres and Loranca. In other work, Mera turns design obstacles to advantage. In a commercial housing block in Las Rosas, Madrid, for example, he used a last-minute change in permitted density to carve a series of double-height terraces out of the volume.

The Pozuelo Seniors' Center is an interesting product of this struggle, a collage of several incomplete and improvised interventions, which nevertheless come together in an intriguing spatial sequence. Its labyrinthine, incremental composition, common to large institutions that have grown over time, offers eccentric pleasures that are perhaps unfairly under-valued in contemporary architecture.

Während ein Großteil der Architekturdebatte in Spanien kaum über die beschränkten Zirkel der Zunft und das hinausgeht, was Manilla & Tuñón als „Gespräche in gedämpftem Ton" bezeichnen, lebt Juan Ignacio Mera in der harten Welt des kommerziellen Bauens, im täglichen Kampf um die Gunst von Auftraggebern, Generalunternehmern und Öffentlichkeit, und im Einklang mit den strengen Prinzipien seiner Ausbildung an der Architekturfakultät Madrid.

Mera unterhält einen Angestelltenstab von über 12 Architekten und hat einen großen Auftragsbestand von staatlich geförderten und kommerziellen Wohngebäuden sowie Geschäftshäusern und öffentlichen Einrichtungen. Er arbeitet alleine oder mit anderen zusammen. Mera sagt, daß er Diskussionen mit den Bauherren über Ästhetik zu vermeiden sucht, doch diese profitierten von seinen hohen Standards, die dem Architekten zum Beispiel den Zuschlag für öffentliche Gebäude von gemeinnützigen Baugesellschaften in Pamplona, Cáceres und Loranca eintrugen. Bei anderen Arbeiten verwandelt Mera Gestaltungshindernisse in einen Vorteil. Bei einem Geschäftshausblock in Las Rosas, Madrid, benutzte er zum Beispiel eine in letzter Minute vorgenommene Änderung der erlaubten Bebauungsdichte dazu, eine Reihe von Terrassen in doppelter Geschoßhöhe aus dem Volumen zu schneiden.

Das Seniorenzentrum Pozuelo ist ein interessantes Produkt dieses schwierigen Prozesses, eine Collage mehrerer unvollständiger und improvisierter Eingriffe, die sich dennoch zu einer berückenden Raumsequenz verbinden. Seine irrgartenhafte, schrittweise zu ergänzende Komposition, die bei großen, über die Zeit gewachsenen Institutionen typisch ist, bereitet ein exzentrisches Vergnügen, das vielleicht in der zeitgenössischen Architektur zu Unrecht zu kurz kommt.

Subsidized Housing Loranca   Fuenlabrada (Madrid), 1995–1997
Gefördertes Wohnungsbauprojekt Loranca

Loranca Garden City is a medium-density public/private development ment outside the Madrid suburb of Fuenlabrada. The project's massing of paired ten-story point towers was determined by the master plan, developed by Equipo Auia Architects. Each tower contains 32 apartments conforming to subsidized housing standards for units of three bedrooms and 70 m². The identical units are arranged in a pinwheel plan around a central void containing elevator and stairs. The plan permits a severe, asymmetrical fenestration, used to counter the symmetry of the master plan's massing.

The structure consists of four concrete shear walls defining the central void, and perimeter columns, producing column-free unit plans that can be changed by owners. Plumbing chases are concentrated at the four corners of the plan. The towers appear to float on the large corner enclosures of the open ground floor, while the projecting metal cornice gives them a vertical termination. The central voids are naturally lit from above, and the rooftop terraces are accessible. The ground floor plaza covers a parking garage.

Die Gartenstadt Loranca ist ein teils staatliches, teils privates Wohnungsbauprojekt im Madrider Vorort Fuenlabrada von mittlerer Bebauungsdichte. Die Untergliederung in paarweise angeordnete zehngeschossige Turmhäuser war vom Masterplan festgelegt, den das Architekturbüro Equipo Auia entwikkelte. Jeder Turm enthält 32 Apartments, die den Standards des sozialen Wohnungsbaus für Vier-Zimmer-Wohnungen von 70 m² Größe entsprechen. Die identischen Einheiten sind windmühlenartig um einen Kern herum angelegt, in dem sich Fahrstuhl und Treppenhaus befinden. Der Grundriß erlaubt eine strenge, asymmetrische Verteilung der Fenster, mit der Mera der symmetrischen Mas-

Tower elevation from facing tower
Turmansicht vom gegenüberliegenden Wohnturm aus

Detail, roof and balcony
Dach- und Balkondetail

Plaza level
Vorplatzniveau

Client
 Auftraggeber
Mutual Cooperative of the
National Police

Collaborators
 Mitarbeiter
Estudio Arquitectura MH with
Ricardo Canada, Gustavo
Piqueras Fisk, Pilar Ribera,
Mario Abajo, Cristina Cercadillo,
J. Enrique López

Technical Architect
 Ausführungsplanung
Eloy Vicente

Structural engineer
 Tragwerk
Julio García Maroto

Mechanical engineer
 Haustechnik
Carbonell Engineers, S. L.

Builder
 Generalunternehmer
ADRA S.A.

Chief of works
 Bauleiter
Esteban Loeches

Photos
 Fotos
Eduardo Sánchez &
Ángel Luis Baltanás

senverteilung des Masterplan entgegenwirkt. Das Skelett besteht aus vier Betonwandscheiben, die den Kern definieren, sowie Stützen entlang des äußeren Gebäuderandes, so daß die Wohnungsgrundrisse stützenfrei bleiben und von den Eigentümern geändert werden können. Die Schächte für die Wasserleitungen konzentrieren sich an den vier Ecken des Grundrisses. Die Türme scheinen über den großen Eckelementen des offenen Erdgeschosses zu schweben, während ihnen das auskragende Gesims aus Metall einen Abschluß nach oben gibt. Die Gebäudekerne werden von oben mit natürlichem Licht versorgt, die Dachterrassen sind zugänglich. Unter dem Vorplatz auf dem Niveau des Erdgeschosses befindet sich eine Tiefgarage.

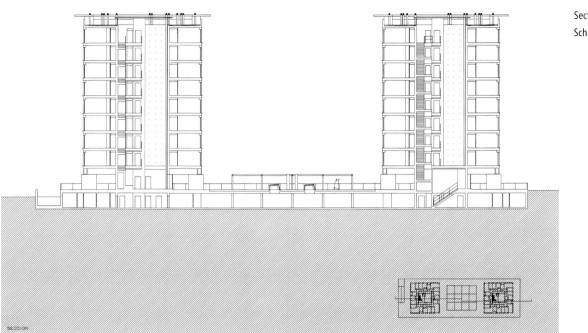

Section

Schnitt

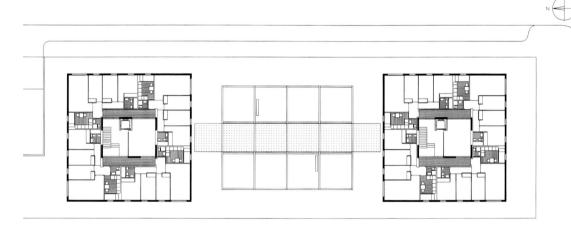

Typical floor plan

Grundriß Regelgeschoß

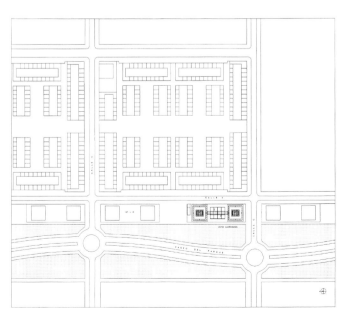

Site plan

Lageplan

49

Fisk House   Valdemorillo (Madrid), 1995
Haus Fisk

General view from south
Gesamtansicht von Süden

South elevation, windows shuttered
Südfassade mit geschlossenen Fensterläden

This modest residence is located in the rugged foothills of the sierra north of Madrid. Contrary to our expectations, the roof rises over the bedrooms, and not the living area. Its sloping plane is uninterrupted in the interiors, rising over bedroom walls and an upper loft located above the master bedroom.

The entry is located on the northern facade. The rooms open to the south, including a large terrace off the living area, defined by a raised platform and a steel frame. The separation of this elevated metallic frame from the solid masonry volume of the house recalls the floating terrace of Alejandro de la Sota's 1975 Dominguez House in La Caeyra (Pontevedra). Sliding wood shutters cover all openings, allowing the house to be completely closed, a typical measure for such isolated locations.

Dieses bescheidene Wohnhaus liegt in den zerklüfteten Vorbergen der Sierra nördlich von Madrid. Anders als man erwarten würde, erhebt sich das Dach über den einzelnen Zimmern, nicht über dem Wohnbereich. Seine schräge Fläche wird im Inneren nicht unterbrochen, erhebt sich über die einzelnen Zimmer und ein Loft über dem Elternschlafzimmer.

Der Eingang liegt an der Nordfassade. Die Räume öffnen sich nach Süden, einschließlich einer großen Terrasse, die vom Wohnbereich abgeht und durch eine erhobene und mit einem Stahlrahmen versehene Plattform definiert ist. Die Trennung dieses erhöhten Metallrahmens vom massiven Mauerwerk des Baukörpers erinnert an die schwebende Terrasse von Alejandro de la Sotas Haus Dominguez von 1975 in La Caeyra (Pontevedra). Hölzerne Schiebefensterläden bedecken alle Öffnungen. Mit ihnen kann das Haus – eine typische Maßnahme an solch isolierten Wohnorten – völlig verschlossen werden.

Porch
Veranda

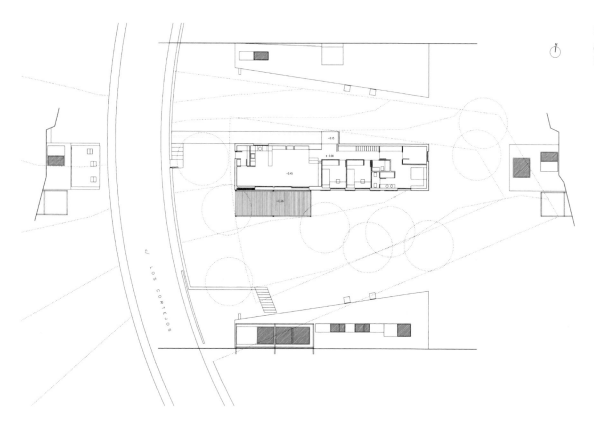

Main floor plan, elevations
Grundriß und Aufrisse
Hauptgeschoß

Living room
Wohnzimmer

Client
 Auftraggeber
Carlota Fisk Godoy

Collaborators
 Mitarbeiter
Javier Pérez de Lucas,
Gustavo Piqueras Fisk

Technical architect
 Ausführungsplanung
Florencio Gutiérrez

Builder
 Generalunternehmer
Belocón S.A

Photos
 Fotos
Eduardo Sánchez &
Ángel Luis Baltanás

Seniors' Center Pozuelo de Alarcón (Madrid), 1989–1998
Seniorenzentrum

Model, 1989 volume

Modellansicht des Vorbaus
von 1989

Client
  Auftraggeber
Municipality of Pozuelo de
Alarcón

Collaborating designer
  Mitarbeit am Entwurf, Phase I
Jesús San Vicente

Collaborators
  Mitarbeiter
Estudio Arquitectura MH

Technical architect
  Kostenkontrolle
Florencio Gutiérrez

Builders
  Generalunternehmer
Phase I, Atocha
Phase II, Teodoro Santamaria
Phase III, Aniceto Castiblanque

The project developed in an ad-hoc manner over ten years. The portico, with a social activities room above, was commissioned in 1989 to terminate the fourth side of the town square, opposite the postwar town hall. Mera's marble-clad volume and clock tower recall the planned rural settlements of J. L. Fernández del Amo of the 1950s, and their modernism inspired in vernacular forms. The stair volume behind the portico is crowned by a decorative tower clad in metal panels and housing mechanical installations.

In the second phase, existing one-story volumes behind the portico were rehabilitated, and in the third phase, a large exercise room/assembly hall was added at the back of the site. The new volume is executed in exposed concrete, and receives natural light from the patio and rooftop monitors. The repeated metal plaques of its street facade recall the shell reliefs of Salamanca's medieval Casa de las Conchas, a device designed to give the facade texture and weight in response to a nearby church.

The Center is entered from the portico, where a door in the rear wall opens to one of the patios, or from the stair tower. Rehabilitated wings contain offices, dressing rooms, a first aid center, workshops and a cafeteria.

Das Projekt wurde in mehreren Schritten über einen Zeitraum von zehn Jahren entwickelt. Der Vorbau mit einem Raum für Gemeinschaftsaktivitäten darüber wurde 1989 in Auftrag gegeben, um die vierte Seite des Stadtplatzes gegenüber dem Rathaus aus der Nachkriegszeit abzuschließen. Meras marmorverkleidetes Volumen mit Glockenturm erinnert an die von J. L. Fernández del Amo geplanten ländlichen Siedlungen aus den 50er Jahren und ihren von lokalen Formen inspirierten Modernismus. Das Treppenhausvolumen hinter dem Vorbau krönt ein dekorativer, mit Metallpaneelen verkleideter Turm, in dem die Haustechnik untergebracht ist.

Im zweiten Bauabschnitt wurden vorhandene eingeschossige Baukörper hinter dem Vorbau renoviert und im dritten wurde auf dem hinteren Grundstücksteil ein großer Übungs- und Versammlungssaal hinzugefügt. Der neue Bauteil ist in Sichtbeton ausgeführt und erhält natürliches Licht vom Hof und den Oberlichtern. Die sich wiederholenden Metallplatten seiner Straßenfassade erinnern an die Muschelreliefs der mittelalterlichen Casa de las Conchas in Salamanca und sollen der Fassade in bezug auf eine nahe Kirche Textur und Gewicht geben.

Das Zentrum betritt man durch den Portikus, wo sich eine Tür in der hinteren Wand zu einem der Innenhöfe öffnet, oder vom Treppenhausturm aus. Die sanierten Flügel beherbergen Büros, Umkleideräume, eine Erste-Hilfe-Station, Werkstätten und eine Cafeteria.

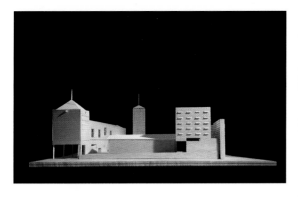

1998 addition and patio
Anbau von 1998 und Innenhof

1998 addition, interior at street facade
Anbau von 1998, Innenraum an der Seite zur Straße

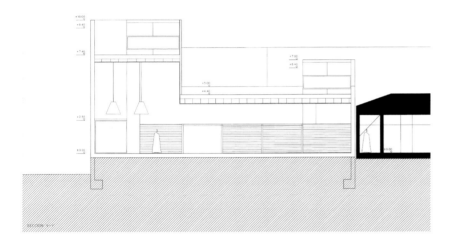

Section, 1998 addition
Schnitt durch den Anbau von 1998

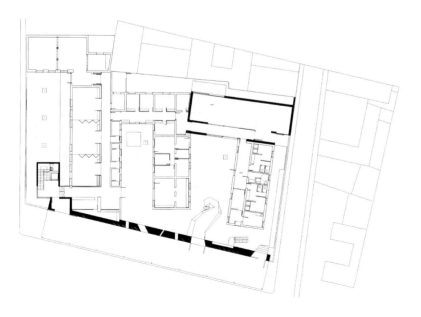

Ground floor plan
Grundriß Erdgeschoß

Foreign Office Architects London
Alejandro Zaera & Farshid Moussavi

Alejandro Zaera, born and trained in Madrid and with close ties to Spain through his professional, writing and teaching activities, met Farshid Moussavi in a Masters program at Harvard. After working for Rem Koolhaas in Rotterdam during two years, the couple moved to London in 1993 to become Unit Masters at the Architectural Association. They established Foreign Office Architects (FOA) at the same time, on the experimental premise of developing a trans-national, critical practice. The firm won its first international recognition in 1995 with the competition-winning design for the Yokohama Ship Terminal.

The architects take their strategic position as foreigners in London as an emblem of their critical stance. Of his first year in the United States, Zaera recalls, "All the knowledge that I had accumulated, with all of its certainties, suddenly disappeared. It is as if the ground under your feet begins to move, and you don't know very well where you are stepping. This is what interests us, to confront unknown realities as a creative process, to operate outside a context with clear and closed rules. To have to, in every moment, construct the terrain over which you move." In contrast to the restrained De la Sotian designs of many of their Spanish peers, the work that results from this creative strategy is protean and metamorphic in nature, open to suggestive visual allusions and unexpected formal strategies, and charged with a sense of risk and adventure.

Alejandro Zaera wurde in Madrid geboren und ausgebildet und unterhält durch seine berufliche Arbeit, sein Schreiben und seine Lehrtätigkeit enge Beziehungen nach Spanien. Er lernte Farshid Moussavi bei einem Graduierten-Programm an der Universität von Harvard kennen. Nachdem sie zwei Jahre lang für Rem Koolhaas in Rotterdam gearbeitet hatten, zog das Paar 1993 nach London, um an der Architectural Association zu unterrichten. Gleichzeitig gründeten sie Foreign Office Architects (FOA) mit der experimentellen Zielsetzung, eine länderübergreifende kritische Praxis zu entwickeln. Das Büro errang 1995 erste internationale Anerkennung, als sie mit ihrem Entwurf den Wettbewerb für den Yokohama Schiffshafen gewann.

Für die Architekten ist ihre Stellung als Ausländer in London ein Sinnbild ihrer kritischen Position. Zaera erinnert sich an sein erstes Jahr in den USA: „Alles Wissen, das ich erworben hatte, mit all seinen Gewißheiten, verschwand plötzlich. Das ist, als ob der Boden unter den Füßen zu wanken beginnt und man nicht mehr genau weiß, wohin man treten soll. Das ist es, was uns interessiert: die Begegnung mit unbekannten Realitäten als kreativer Prozeß, die Arbeit außerhalb eines Kontextes mit klaren und geschlossenen Regeln; in jedem Moment das Terrain erst schaffen zu müssen, über das man geht." Im Gegensatz zu den zurückhaltenden Entwürfen vieler ihrer Altersgenossen im Stile De la Sotas ist die Arbeit, die sich aus dieser kreativen Strategie ergibt, ihrem Wesen nach wandelbar und vielgestaltig, ist offen für stimulierende visuelle Anregungen und unerwartete formale Strategien und aufgeladen mit einem Gefühl des Risikos und Abenteuers.

International Ship Terminal Yokohama Japan 1995 –
Internationaler Schiffshafen

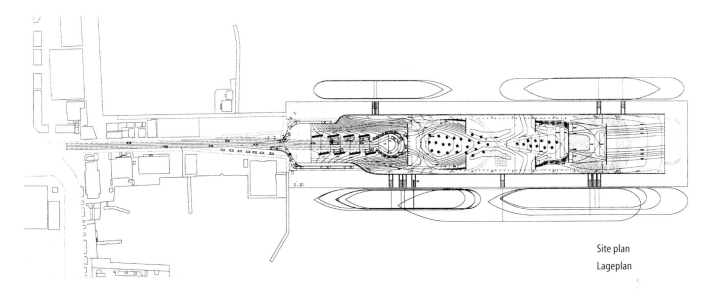

Site plan
Lageplan

The architects conceived the 48,000 m² terminal pier as "an extension of the urban ground" in the form of a continuous folded surface, a complex topological figure which splits and opens and doubles back on itself to produce "an uninterrupted and multi-directional spatial flow." The shifting levels of the terminal proper, an area of shops and restaurants, and a conference area and exhibition hall, are interconnected among themselves and with the land-side vehicular drop-off, the lower-level parking garage and the upper plaza.

This folded surface is structurally self-supporting. Instead of using conventional vertical columns, loads are displaced laterally along the surface of the folded slabs. This apparently inefficient system is justified by seismic design requirements, in which gravitational loads are often secondary to lateral forces. The resulting structure, symmetrical about its longitudinal axis, has an organic quality, like the thin-shell concrete structures of the 1960s. Mouth-like ramps open on the upper surface of the plaza or within the large interior concourses to connect different levels, points of deformation on the folded surface at which structural stresses are also concentrated.

Die Architekten konzipierten den 48.000 m² großen Pier als „eine Erweiterung des urbanen Raumes" in Form einer kontinuierlichen gefalteten Fläche, eine komplexe topologische Figur, die sich spaltet, öffnet und übereinanderschiebt, um „einen ununterbrochenen räumlichen Fluß in viele Richtungen" zu schaffen. Die versetzten Ebenen der eigentlichen Hafenanlage, ein Bereich für Läden und Restaurants und ein Konferenzzentrum mit Ausstellungshalle sind miteinander und mit der landseitigen Zufahrt, der Parkgarage auf der unteren Ebene und der oberen Plaza verbunden.

Diese gefaltete Fläche ist eine frei tragende Konstruktion. Statt konventionelle vertikale Stützen zu benutzen, wird die Last seitlich entlang der Fläche der gefalteten Platten nach unten geführt. Dieses scheinbar ineffiziente System rechtfertigt sich durch die im Entwurf zu berücksichtigenden Auflagen zum Erdbebenschutz, bei denen vertikale Lasten häufig gegenüber lateralen Kräften zweitrangig sind. Die daraus resultierende Konstruktion, die entlang ihrer Längsachse symmetrisch ist, hat eine organische Qualität, wie die dünnen Betonschalen der 60er Jahre. Rampen öffnen sich wie Münder auf die obere Plaza oder innerhalb der großen inneren Hallen, um verschiedene Ebenen zu verbinden, Orte, an denen sich die gefaltete Fläche verformt und sich auch die konstruktiven Lasten konzentrieren.

Rendering
Zeichnung

Client
  Auftraggeber
City of Yokohama

I. Competition

Collaborators
  Mitarbeiter
I. Ascanio, Y-K. Chong, M. Cosmas,
J-H Hwang, G. Westbrook

Engineers
  Tragwerk
Ove Arup & Partners

Models
  Modelle
Andrew Ingham Associates

II. Basic design

Collaborators
  Mitarbeiter
K. Matsuzawa, S. Triginer,
J. Mansilla, F. Bendito,
M. Company, M. Monterde

Co-architects
  Mitarchitekten
GKK Architects, Japan

Structural engineer
  Statik
Structural Design Group, Japan

Mechanical engineer
  Haustechnik
P.T. Morimura, Japan

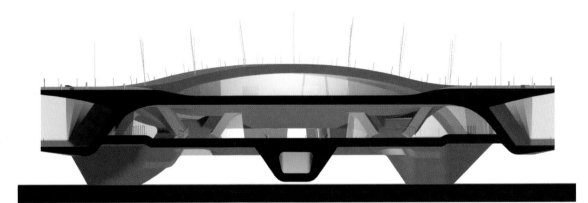

Cross section, restaurant,
shopping area
Querschnitt Restaurant,
Einkaufsareal

Detail, cross section
Detailschnitt

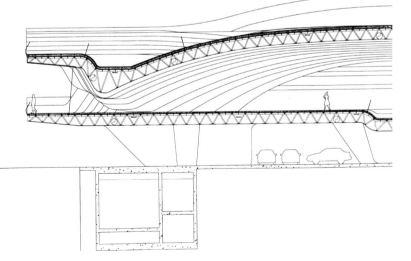

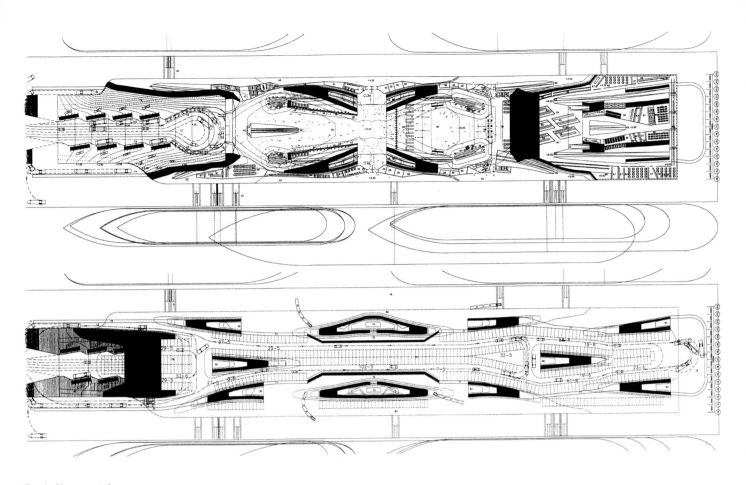

Terminal/restaurant plan,
level +5.00

Grundriß Hafengebäude/
Restaurant, Niveau +5.00

Parking plan, level +0.00

Grundriß Parkplätze,
Niveau +0.00

Longitudinal section A-A

Längsschnitt A-A

Longitudinal section B-B

Längsschnitt B-B

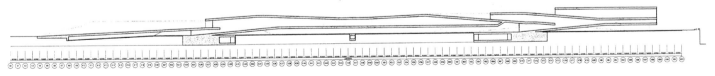

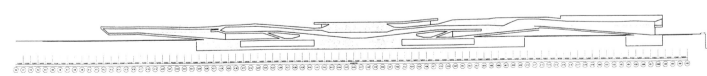

Link Quay Redevelopment   Santa María de Tenerife, Canary Islands 1997–1998
Umgestaltung Verbindungsmole im Hafen

Aerial view
Luftbild

Client
  Auftraggeber
Port Authority of Tenerife

Collaborators
  Mitarbeiter
K. Matsuzawa, L. Ortega, L. Falcón,
N. Ninomiya, Ch. Ag-Ukrikul, J.
Gálmez, M. Ansari, L. Jensen

Structural engineer
  Statik
Adams Kara Taylor, London

Environmental engineering
  Umwelttechnik
BDSP, London

Landscape architect
  Landschaftsarchitekt
Karres & Brandt; Hilversum,
Holland

Traffic consultants
  Verkehrsplanung
Halcrow Fox, London

For the reconversion of the city's obsolete port area to recreational and urban uses, FOA proposed a variation on the Yokohama Terminal structure. In this case, the central "link quay," which connects the city to an outer line of breakwater-piers, is developed as a non-symmetrical multi-layered surface of flowing, interweaving horizontal bands. These linear bands are supported by a flexible, repeatable system of tilted and inter-crossed prefabricated columns.

The link quay structure contains a shopping center, restaurants, cinemas and parking. The urban edge of the surrounding port area is lined with smaller structures based on the same elements, and containing sports facilities, a marina, and the like. These pier-like elements extend the city streets over the lower existing port area and a circulation artery to the waterside. The architects see their intervention as an urban infrastructure more than an urban design, in that it offers a flexible and repeatable system into which program elements can be inserted according to developing demand.

Für die Umwandlung des alten Hafenareals für Erholungszwecke und urbane Nutzungen schlugen FOA eine Variation der Hafenkonstruktion von Yokohama vor. In diesem Fall entwickelten sie die zentrale „Verbindungsmole", die die Stadt mit einer äußeren Linie von Kais verbindet, als nicht-symmetrische, vielschichtige Fläche aus fließenden, ineinander verwobenen horizontalen Bändern. Diese linearen Bänder ruhen auf einem flexiblen, erweiterbaren System von geneigten und gekreuzten vorgefertigten Stützen.

In der Verbindungsmole befinden sich ein Einkaufszentrum, Restaurants, Kinos und Parkplätze. Die stadtzugewandte Ecke des umliegenden Hafenareals ist von kleineren Bauten gesäumt, die auf den gleichen Elementen basieren. Dazu gehören Sporteinrichtungen, ein Yachthafen und ähnliches. Diese pierartigen Elemente verlängern die städtischen Straßen über das vorhandene untere Hafenareal und eine Schnellstraße hinweg zum Wasser. Die Architekten sehen ihr Projekt eher als eine urbane Infrastruktur denn als eine fertige urbane Gestaltung, bietet es doch ein flexibles und addierbares System, in das sich je nach wachsenden Erfordernissen weitere Programmelemente einfügen lassen.

View from sea
Ansicht vom Meer aus

Layout plan
Lageplan

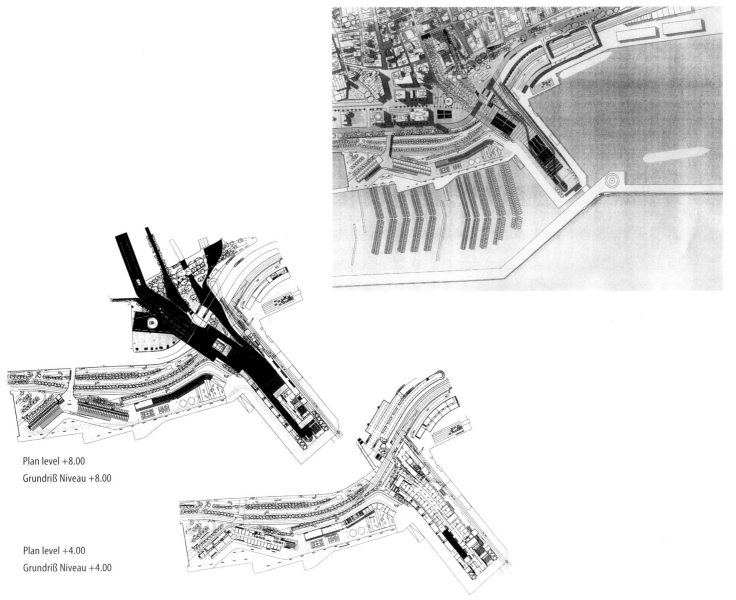

Plan level +8.00
Grundriß Niveau +8.00

Plan level +4.00
Grundriß Niveau +4.00

Belgo Zuid Restaurant   Notting Hill Gate, London 1999
Belgo Zuid Restaurant

View from 1st floor
Ansicht vom Obergeschoß aus

Client
  Auftraggeber
Belgo Group PL

Collaborators
  Mitarbeiter
M. Morrish, K. Matsuzawa,
Xavier Ortiz, Lluis Viu

Structural engineer
  Statik
Adams Kara Taylor, London

Mechanical engineer
  Haustechnik
John Brady Associates, London

Quantity surveyors
  Kontrolle
Leslie Clark, London

FOA was asked to provide architectural services for the New York, London and Bristol (UK) branches of a Belgian restaurant chain (interior furnishings are by others). According to the architects, their designs "play with the 'themes' of the chain, exploiting them as forms, structures and organizations beyond their kitsch origins. Mussel shells, velodromes, stomachs, beer barrels, stained glass windows, medieval vaults and Brueghel become our arguments for producing architecture."

In London's Ladbroke Grove project, they replaced much of a small, deteriorated theater with a shell-like structure of stainless steel vaults, broken by curving skylights and lined on the inside in oak. The kitchen, located behind the former proscenium, is visible from the dining room. Its infrared lighting and stainless steel surfaces are designed in vertiginous contrast with the blue neon lighting of the mezzanine bar above it, to suggest "a medieval diptych representing heaven and hell, as in Hieronymus Bosch." The narrow streetfront

FOA wurde gebeten, die Architektur der Filialen einer belgischen Restaurantkette in New York, London und Bristol (Großbritannien) zu übernehmen (die Innenausstattung entwarfen andere). Ihre Entwürfe, so die Architekten, "spielen mit den 'Themen' der Kette, indem sie von ihren Ursprüngen im Kitsch absehen und ihr Formen-, Konstruktions- und Organisationspotential ausloten. Muscheln, Velodrome, Mägen, Bierfässer, Buntglasfenster, mittelalterliche Gewölbe und Breughel werden zu unseren Argumenten, Architektur zu schaffen".

Beim Projekt in Ladbroke Grove in London ersetzten sie den Großteil eines kleinen, heruntergekommenen Theaters durch eine schalenartige Konstruktion aus Edelstahlkuppeln, die durch gewölbte Oberlichter unterbrochen werden und an der Innenseite mit Eichenholz verkleidet sind. Die Küche hinter der ehemaligen Vorbühne ist vom Speisesaal aus sichtbar. Ihre Infrarotbeleuchtung und Edelstahlflächen stehen in massivem Kontrast zur blauen Neonbeleuchtung der Bar im Zwischengeschoß darüber, um "ein mittelalterliches Diptychon" nahe-

60

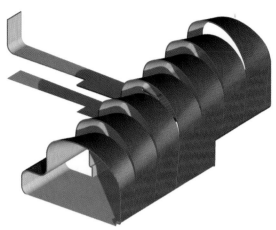

Main dining hall
Restaurantbereich

Conceptual axonometric
Konzeptionelle Axonometrie

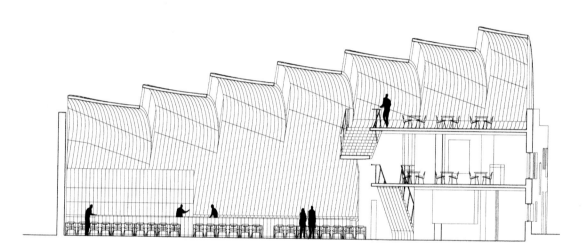

Section
Schnitt

is covered by a 12-meter high sign, with alternating messages produced by rotating louvers. The entry passage, 20 meters long and 3 meters wide, is lined with beer bottles.

In New York, the floors and ceiling of a long narrow space are finished in a discontinuous tubular surface composed of synthetic resin, which draws on images of intestines, sausages, the New York subway, highways, an airplane, etc.

zulegen, das „wie bei Hieronymus Bosch Himmel und Hölle darstellt". Die schmale Straßenfront ist von einer 12 Meter hohen Anzeigentafel bedeckt, die mit rotierenden Lamellen wechselnde Werbebilder zeigt. Die 20 Meter lange und drei Meter breite Eingangspassage ist mit Bierflaschen gesäumt.

In New York nehmen Fußboden und Decke eines langen, schmalen Raumes die Form einer diskontinuierlichen Röhre aus Kunstharz an, die an Bilder von Innereien, Würste, die New Yorker U-Bahn, Autobahnen oder Flugzeuge erinnert.

61

Manuel Ruisánchez & Xavier Vendrell   Barcelona

Manuel Ruisánchez and Xavier Vendrell received their formative experience in two key centers of Barcelona's urban regeneration. Coinciding in the studio of E. Torres and J.A. Martínez-Lapeña at different times, they worked on projects such as the Villa Cecilia Gardens (1982–86). Their collaboration began in the city architecture department, as members of the young team recruited by Oriol Bohigas to execute the famed parks and plazas program. The competition-winning design for the Poblenou Park and Marbella Pavilion permitted them to open an independent studio in 1988. Like colleagues E. Batlle & J. Roig, their experience in landscape design afforded them extra opportunities in a region dominated by architects of an older generation. It has also influenced their design philosophy, as developed from Torres and Martínez-Lapeña. They summarize their approach in the idea that "Architecture and its setting are part of a single whole." They look beyond formal issues for the conceptual core of each problem, or what they call its "hard-core temperament." In the mixing of buildings and outdoor spaces of the Riumar School, for example, the design is organized by horizontal rooflines that structure alternating solids and voids at various scales. This compositional pattern arose from a careful study of the site. "We wanted to avoid introducing a foreign body into the landscape. We tried to read the rules of the game proposed by the place, and take off from there."

Manuel Ruisánchez und Xavier Vendrell erhielten ihre Ausbildung in zwei Zentren der Stadterneuerung Barcelonas. Beide waren zu verschiedenen Zeiten Mitarbeiter des Architekturbüros von Torres und Martínez-Lapeña und arbeiteten dort an Projekten wie den Gärten der Villa Cecilia (1982–1986). Ihre Zusammenarbeit begann im Bauressort der Stadt als Mitglieder des jungen Teams, das Oriol Bohigas zusammenstellte, um das berühmte Bauprogramm der Parks und Plätze durchzuführen. Der erste Preis bei den Wettbewerben für den Poblenou Park mit der Marbella-Halle erlaubte ihnen, 1988 ein unabhängiges Architekturbüro zu eröffnen.

Wie bei ihren Kollegen Enric Batlle und Joan Roig eröffnete ihnen ihre Erfahrung mit Landschaftsarchitektur zusätzliche Möglichkeiten in einem Bereich, der von Architekten einer älteren Generation bestimmt wurde. Diese Erfahrung beeinflußte auch ihre Entwurfsphilosophie, die auf Torres' und Martínez-Lapeñas Architektur aufbaut. Sie fassen ihren Ansatz in dem Gedanken zusammen, daß „Architektur und ihr Kontext Teil eines Ganzen sind". Sie suchen über formale Fragen hinaus nach dem konzeptionellen Kern jedes Problems, nach dem, was sie sein „eigentliches Temperament" nennen. Bei der Riumar-Schule zum Beispiel organisieren horizontale Dachlinien die alternierende Mischung von Körpern und Räumen in unterschiedlichen Dimensionen. Dieses Kompositionsmuster entstand aus einer sorgfältigen Studie des Ortes. „Wir wollten vermeiden, einen Fremdkörper in die Landschaft zu setzen. Wir haben versucht, die Regeln zu begreifen, die der Ort selbst nahelegte, und sie zu unserem Ausgangspunkt zu machen."

Poblenou Park, Poblenou   Barcelona, 1988–1992
Poblenou Park

Aerial view from Olympic Village
Luftbild vom Olympischen Dorf aus

Boardwalk over sand dunes
Die Uferpromenade oberhalb der Sanddünen

The park is an extension of the complex operation carried out at the adjacent Olympic Village to the west. It involves the reconversion of obsolete industrial land for new beaches and gardens, including the Marbella Pavilion and athletic field. The narrow border between the working class neighborhood of Poblenou and the sea is layered in thin spatial zones: the urban facade of Poblenou, the landscaped borders of the depressed coastal highway, gardens of dunes anchored by local vegetation and banks of low coastal pines, a zone of intense public use, and the seaside boardwalk. The high-use zone includes playing fields, playgrounds, outdoor cafes and an open area for popular festivities. Straight paths perpendicular to the water continue the trajectory of inland streets, while curving longitudinal paths follow the topography. Different types of night lighting distinguish different paths and zones, including light towers designed by the architects for high-use areas. The grounds are watered by a system of sprinklers on tall masts that simulate rainfall, a method that reduces the effects of the salinity in the air and soil.

Der Park ist die Erweiterung eines komplexen Projektes für das westlich angrenzende Olympische Dorf. Dazu gehörte die Rückgewinnung ehemaliger Gewerbeflächen, auf denen neue Strände und Gärten, der Marbella-Pavillon und ein Sportplatz entstanden.

Das schmale Areal zwischen dem Arbeiterviertel Poblenou und dem Meer ist in streifenförmige räumliche Zonen gegliedert: der städtische Bereich von Poblenou, die landschaftlich gestalteten Ränder der tiefliegenden Küstenautobahn, mit örtlicher Vegetation und niedrigen Küstenpinien befestigte Dünengärten, eine Zone intensiver öffentlicher Nutzung und eine Uferpromenade. Zur öffentlichen Zone gehören Sport- und Spielplätze, Caféterrassen und ein offenes Veranstaltungsareal.

Gerade Wege rechtwinklig zur Uferlinie verlängern die zum Meer führenden Straßen, während quer dazu gewundene Wege dem Geländeprofil folgen. Verschiedene Beleuchtungssysteme markieren verschiedene Wege und Zonen, darunter Lichttürme, die die Architekten eigens für die intensiv genutzten Areale entwarfen. Der Boden wird durch ein System von Sprinklern auf hohen Masten bewässert, eine Nachahmung des natürlichen Niederschlags, durch die der Salzgehalt in Luft und Boden vermindert wird.

Client
_Auftraggeber
Vila Olímpica S.A.

Builder
_Generalunternehmer
ACYSA, Cubiertas y MZOV, Ferrovial, Floret S.A., Rosset

Photos
_Fotos
Mónica Rosilló

Aerial photo
_Luftbild
Tabisa

63

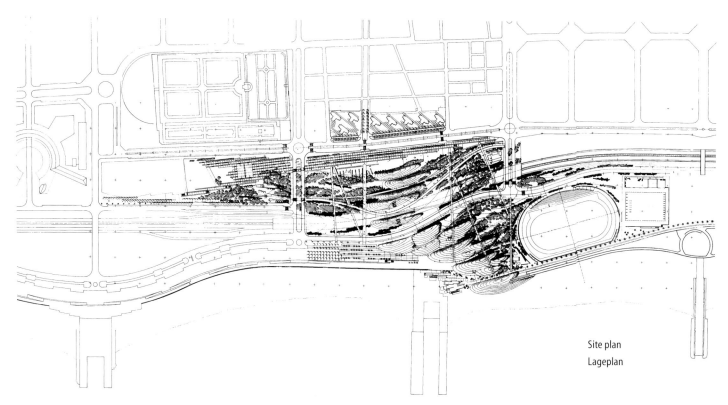

Site plan
Lageplan

Architect-designed light towers

Die von den Architekten
entworfenen Lichttürme

View towards Olympic Village

Blick zum Olympischen Dorf

64

Marbella Pavilion, Poblenou Park   Barcelona, 1988–1992
Marbella-Halle

Entry facade

Exterior detail, perforated Corten steel panels and concrete piers

Eingangsfassade

Außendetail, Paneele aus perforiertem Corten-Stahl und Betonpfeilern

Client
 Auftraggeber
Vila Olímpica S.A.

Consulting Engineers
 Ingenieure
Sumna Engineering

Builder
 Generalunternehmer
Fomento de Construcciones y Contratas

Photos
 Fotos
Mónica Rosilló

The pavilion was built to house the badminton matches of the 1992 Olympics, and to serve subsequently as a local cultural and sports center. The main floor is sunken into the terrain to reduce the facility's impact on the park. Visitors enter the sports hall from the upper level terrace, and descend to the library, exhibition gallery and Poblenou Archives via a sunken patio on the northern side of the site. The dressing rooms to the south of the sports hall exit directly to the athletic field, which is also sunken to protect it from winds. The sports hall, with a capacity for 1000 spectators, is spanned by 50-meter steel trusses supported by precast concrete piers. The interior face of the hall defined by the piers is finished in operable glass, and the exterior in vanes of perforated corten steel above a 2.5 meter-high horizontal band of clear glass. Skylights located between piers bring natural light to the lower floor. End elevations are finished in plywood panels.

Die Halle wurde für die Badmintonspiele der Olympiade von 1992 gebaut, um danach als Kultur- und Sportzentrum zu dienen. Das Hauptgeschoß ist abgesenkt, damit das Gebäude im Park nicht zu dominant wird. Besucher betreten die Sporthalle von der oberen Terrasse und gelangen über einen abgesenkten Hof an der Nordseite des Grundstücks zur Bibliothek, dem Ausstellungsbereich und dem Poblenou-Archiv. Die Umkleideräume im südlichen Teil der Halle führen direkt auf ein Spielfeld, das ebenfalls tiefer liegt, damit es vor Wind geschützt ist.

Die Sporthalle mit ihrer Kapazität von 1000 Zuschauerplätzen wird von 50 Meter langen Stahlträgern überspannt, die auf vorgefertigten Betonpfeilern ruhen. Die von den Pfeilern definierte Innenfassade der Halle besteht aus Glaselementen, die sich öffnen lassen, die Außenfassade aus perforierten Corten-Stahlstreifen über einem 2,5 Meter hohen horizontalen Band aus Klarsichtglas. Oberlichter zwischen den Pfeilern versorgen das untere Geschoß mit natürlichem Licht. Die Endfassaden sind mit Sperrholzpaneelen verkleidet.

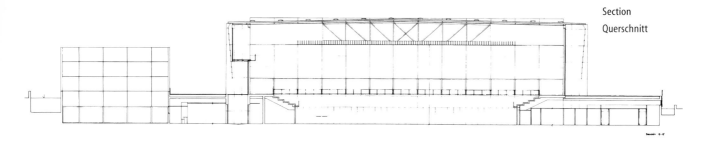

Section
Querschnitt

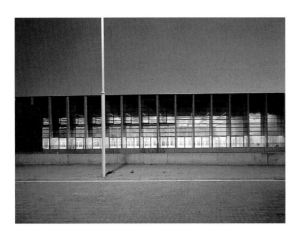

Side elevation at dusk
Seitenfassade in der Dämmerung

Facade from interior
Fassade von innen

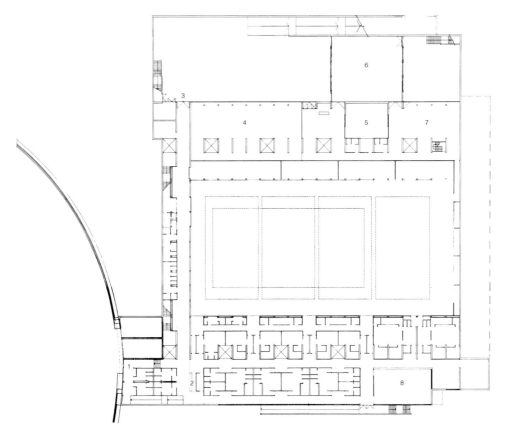

Lower level plan
Grundriß Untergeschoß

1 Exit, athletic field
  Ausgang, Sportfeld
2 Dressing room control
  Umkleideraumaufsicht
3 Vehicular access
  Zufahrt
4 Library
  Bibliothek
5 Auditorium
  Auditorium
6 Exhibition gallery
  Ausstellungsgalerie
7 Poblenou Archives
  Poblenou-Archiv
8 Small gym
  Kleine Turnhalle

Riumar School   Deltebre (Tarragona), 1993–1996
Riumar-Schule

General view from north
Gesamtansicht von Norden

View towards gym from classroom wing
Blick zur Turnhalle von den Klassentrakten

The school is set amid marshy fields and rice patties in the delta of the Ebro River. The warm climate permitted the dispersion of program elements in separate structures that partially enclose and define outdoor spaces, including the primary circulation. Spaces and buildings are oriented towards the south and southeast to avoid the western sun and the prevailing northwest winds of the mistral. Four free-standing wings of classrooms are arranged at the south of the site near the entry court, and linked by an outdoor linear canopy. Separate buildings for the administration, mechanical plant and gymnasium line the northwest border of the parcel. The large space defined between classrooms and gymnasium becomes a point of assembly and center of gravity for the complex. The classrooms are built of prefabricated concrete. Windows are screened by precast concrete louvers to create a sense of privacy and concentration, while open clerestories illuminate the ceilings. Walls are finished in simple planes of wood veneer, blackboard slate, and cork. Each classroom wing ends in an open porch that can accommodate future expansions.

Die Schule liegt inmitten von Marschland und Reisfeldern im Delta des Ebro. Das warme Klima erlaubt die Verteilung des Programms auf separate Bauten, die zum Teil Außenräume umschließen und definieren, darunter das primäre Wegenetz. Räume und Gebäude sind nach Süden und Südosten ausgerichtet, um die Westsonne und die vorherrschenden Nordwestwinde des Mistral zu vermeiden .

Vier freistehende Trakte, in denen die Klassenräume untergebracht sind, gruppieren sich im Süden des Grundstücks nahe dem Eingangshof und sind außen durch einen geraden überdachten Weg miteinander verbunden. Separate Gebäude für die Verwaltung, die Haustechnik und Turnhalle säumen die Nordwestgrenze der Anlage. Der große Bereich zwischen Klassenräumen und Turnhalle ist Versammlungsort und Schwerpunkt des Komplexes.

Die Klassenräume wurden aus vorgefertigten Betonteilen gebaut. Die Fenster sind mit vorgefertigten Betonblenden geschützt, um ein Gefühl der Privatheit und Konzentration zu schaffen, während offene Lichtgaden für eine Belichtung von oben sorgen. Die Wände sind mit schlichtem Holzfurnier, Wandtafeln aus Schiefer und Kork verkleidet. Jeder Klassenraumtrakt stößt an eine offene Kolonnade, an die sich künftige Erweiterungen anschließen lassen.

Client
    Auftraggeber
Department of Education,
Generalitat of Catalunya

Collaborators
    Mitarbeiter
E. Altes, J. Bel, V. Castelló,
Q. Garriga, E. Masclans, V. Rojas,
M. Sola

Technical Architect
    Ausführungsplanung
Eulàlia Aran

Structural engineer
    Tragwerk
JSS Engineering

Builder
    Generalunternehmer
Obras y Servicios Hispania S.A.
(OSHSA)

Photos
    Fotos
Mónica Rosilló

Floor plan
Grundriß

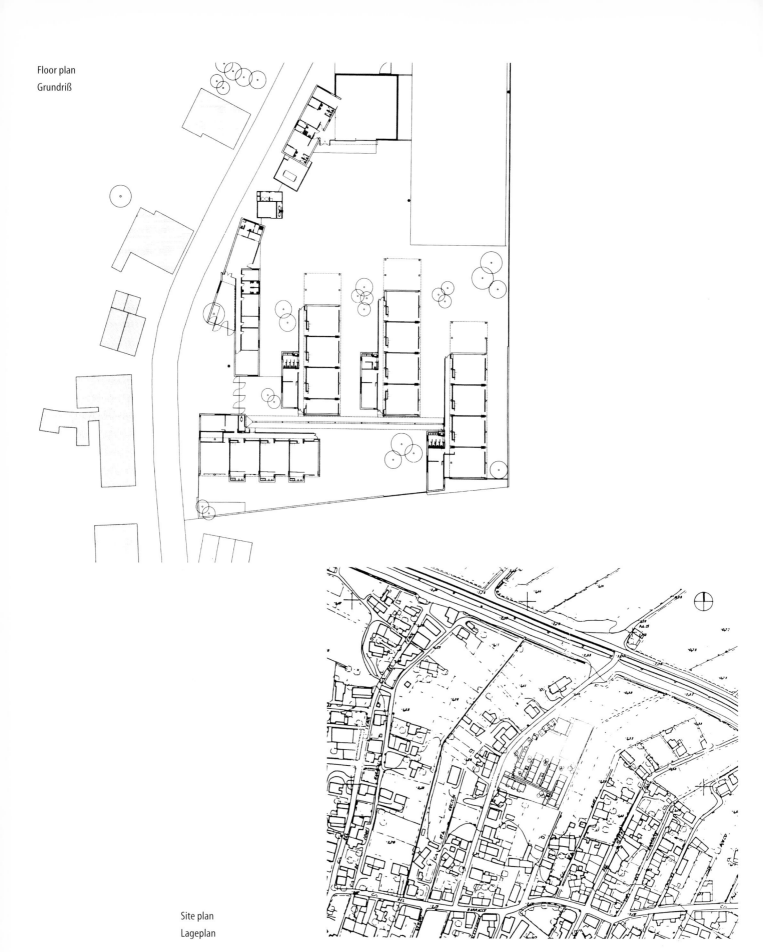

Site plan
Lageplan

Main entry

Haupteingang

Typical classroom interior

Klassenraum

View through window of gym
to classroom wings

Blick durch das Turnhallen-
fenster auf die Klassentrakte

View north between classroom
wings

Blick nach Norden zwischen den
Klassentrakten hindurch

Enric Batlle & Joan Roig   Barcelona

Batlle and Roig gained early recognition for a number of competition-winning landscape designs in Barcelona, such as the Pegaso Park or the Trinitat Cloverleaf Park, located in the center of a highway interchange. But they consider their landscape work as simply another facet of the architectural problem, to be addressed in the same terms as a building using simply a different set of specialized information.

They trace this catholic approach to design to their studies with Rafael Moneo during his years at the Barcelona School of Architecture, and his philosophy of confronting each commission without preconceptions, in a spirit of critical analysis and creative investigation. The thought and teachings of Alejandro de la Sota, as transmitted through their apprenticeship with José A. Martínez Lapeña of the Torres-Martínez Lapeña studio, was another major influence. The eclecticism of the works shown here arises from the limits and issues of each problem. In the Torres-Amat Factory restoration, the intervention was concentrated in a few key elements – mainly the stair and windows – which acquire an exceptional formal intensity. The dissonant window alignments of the Riera Gasulla housing are echoed in the loose organization of buildings around the block, like a shaky freehand line that softens the hard straight edges of public housing standards. And, like the work of their contemporaries Ábalos & Herreros, the Royal Automotive Club takes up the De la Sotian vocabulary of Robertson panels, though with a formal complexity and urbane sophistication in keeping with the image-oriented nature of the corporate commission.

Batlle und Roig errangen frühe Anerkennung mit einer Reihe von ersten Preisen bei Wettbewerben für Landschaftsarchitektur in Barcelona wie den Pegaso Park oder den Trinitat Park, der im Zentrum eines Autobahnkreuzes liegt. Für sie sind ihre Landschaftsgestaltungen nur eine andere Facette der architektonischen Aufgabe, die in gleicher Weise angegangen werden müssen wie ein Gebäude, wobei lediglich eine andere Reihe spezialisierter Informationen zur Anwendung kommt.

Sie führen diesen allgemeingültigen Gestaltungsansatz auf ihre Studienjahre bei Rafael Moneo an der Architekturschule von Barcelona und seine Philosophie zurück, jeden Auftrag im Geist kritischer Analyse und kreativer Erkundung vorurteilslos in Angriff zu nehmen. Das Denken und die Lehre von Alejandro de la Sota, mit denen sie während ihrer Zeit als Mitarbeiter von Martínez Lapeña und Torres in Berührung kamen, war ein anderer wichtiger Einfluß.

Die Hybridität der Werke, die hier vorgestellt werden, entstand aus den Grenzen und Themen jeder Aufgabe. Beim Umbau der Torres-Amat-Fabrik konzentrierte sich der Eingriff auf einige Schlüsselelemente – vor allem die Treppe und die Fenster –, die eine außergewöhnliche formale Intensität gewinnen. Die dissonante Anordnung der Fenster beim Wohnkomplex Riera Gasulla spiegelt sich in der lockeren Organisation der Gebäude um den Block, wie eine von Hand gezogene Linie einer Entwurfszeichnung, die die harten, geraden Ecken des üblichen Sozialwohnungsbaus abmildert. Und wie die Arbeiten ihrer Kollegen Ábalos & Herreros nimmt der Königliche Automobilclub von Batlle und Roig das von De la Sota stammende Vokabular der Robertson-Paneele auf, jedoch mit einer formalen Komplexität und urbanen Verfeinerung, die zum Image der Institution paßt.

Royal Automotive Club of Catalunya   Barcelona, 1990–1996
Königlicher Automobilclub von Katalonien

View from Avenida Diagonal: service station, right; main entry, left

Ansicht von der Avenida Diagonal: rechts Service-Trakt, links Haupteingang

The mixed program of a flagship headquarters and a road service center and gasoline station is reflected in the radical bifurcation of the design, appropriately located at the point where the northeastern highway entrance to Barcelona de-accelerates into the tree-lined urban boulevard of the Diagonal, the city's prestige corporate address. The building is split by a vertical gap between the office tower and gas station, which turn their backs to one another. The site slopes away from the Diagonal to the south, permitting several floors of offices and parking to be located below the entry level. An entry-level terrace at the rear of the site is accessible for car displays and other events, and enjoys views over the city and harbor. The oblique orientation of the tower to the Diagonal follows the precedent set by nearby developments. The tower is divided in a sheer glass-sheathed office zone and a metal-paneled service volume, located so as to shield offices from the afternoon sun. One of the technical challenges of the project was the marriage of different building systems in a unified vertical and horizontal modulation. Exterior finishes include Robertson metal panels, a floor-to-floor glass curtain wall, and exposed poured concrete walls below the entry level.

Perforated metal panels screen the air coolers, which are located on the ground behind the service station so as to make best use of the site's limited zoning envelope.

Das gemischte Programm eines repräsentativen Vereinssitzes mit Pannenhilfe und Tankstelle spiegelt sich in der radikalen Zweiteilung des Gebäudes, das sehr passend an jenem Punkt liegt, wo die nordöstliche Autobahnabfahrt nach Barcelona in den baumgesäumten Boulevard Diagonal übergeht, der besten Geschäftsadresse der Stadt.

Das Gebäude wird von einem vertikalen Einschnitt zwischen dem Büroturm und der Tankstelle, die sich gegenseitig den Rücken zukehren, zweigeteilt. Das Grundstück fällt von der Avenida Diagonal nach Süden hin ab, so daß mehrere Bürogeschosse und die Parkgarage unter dem Niveau des Eingangs liegen können. Eine Terrasse auf dem Niveau des Eingangs im hinteren Grundstücksteil ist für Autoausstellungen und andere Veranstaltungen nutzbar und bietet Ausblicke auf die Stadt und den Hafen. Die schräge Orientierung des Turms zur Diagonal folgt dem Vorbild umliegender Bauten. Der Turm unterteilt sich in eine rein glasverkleidete Bürozone und einen mit Metallpaneelen verkleideten Service-Block, der so gesetzt ist, daß er die Büros vor der Nachmittagssonne abschirmt.

Eine der technischen Herausforderungen des Projektes war die Verbindung verschiedener Konstruktionssysteme in einer einheitlichen vertikalen und horizontalen Modulation. Außen ist das Gebäude unter anderem mit Robertson-Metallpaneelen verkleidet sowie einer gläsernen, jeweils über die volle Geschoßhöhe reichenden Vorhangfassade und Sichtbetonwänden unterhalb des Eingangsniveaus. Perforierte Metallpaneele verblenden die Kühlaggregate, die auf dem Boden hinter dem Service-Block liegen, um die für das Grundstück geltenden baurechtlichen Höhenbeschränkungen bestmöglich zu nutzen.

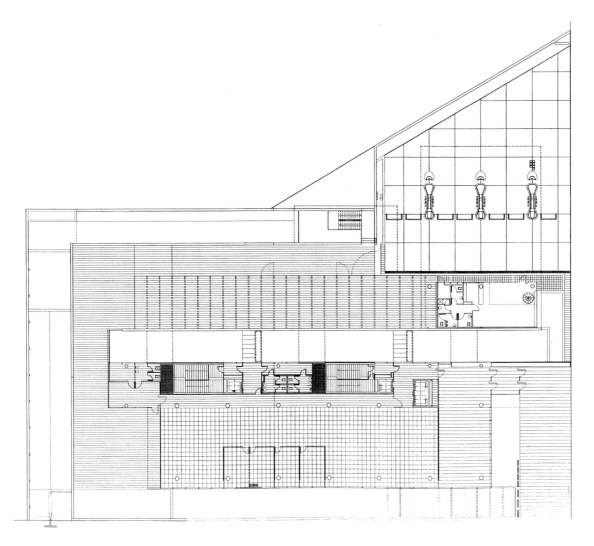

Entry level plan. Service station, upper right, office entry, lower right

Grundriß Eingangsgeschoß. Oben rechts: Pannenhilfe; unten rechts: Büroeingang

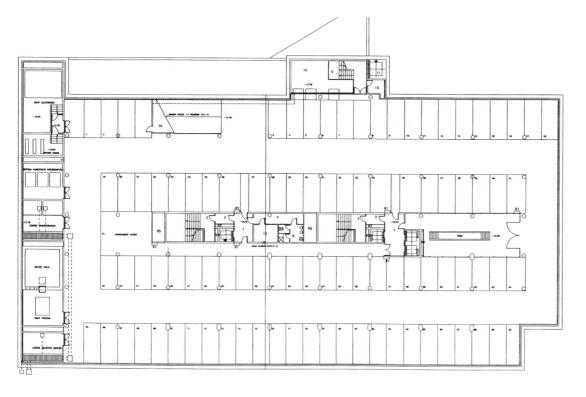

Level -4 plan

Grundriß Niveau -4

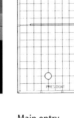

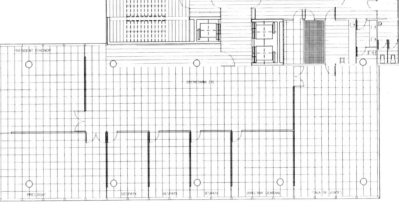

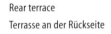

Rear terrace	Entry plaza at Diagonal	Main entry	Service station	Typical tower floor plan
Terrasse an der Rückseite	Eingangsplatz am Boulevard Diagonal	Haupteingang	Pannenhilfe	Grundriß Regelgeschoß des Büroturms

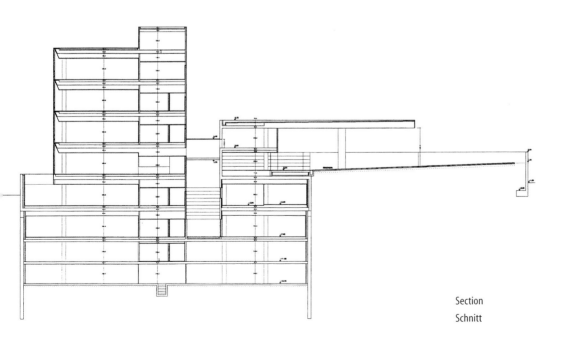

Section

Schnitt

Client
 Auftraggeber
Royal Automotive Club
of Catalunya

Technical architects
 Ausführungsplanung
Lluis Roig, Llibert Moragas

Structural engineer
 Tragwerk
Gerardo Rodríguez

Mechanical engineer
 Haustechnik
Master S.A.

Landscape architect
 Landschaftsarchitect
Teresa Gali

Photos
 Fotos
Jordi Bernardó

Riera Gasulla Subsidized Housing   Sant Boi del Llobregat (Barcelona), 1994–1995
Sozialer Wohnkomplex Riera Gasulla

Central garden
Zentraler Gartenhof

Client
  Auftraggeber
IMPSOL, Metropolitan Area of
Barcelona

Collaborator
  Mitarbeiter
Luis Maldonado

Technical architects
  Ausführungsplanung
Luis Fontanet, Rafael Delgado

Structural engineer
  Tragwerk
Gerardo Rodríguez

Mechanical engineer
  Haustechnik
Técnicas Reunidas

Builder
  Generalunternehmer
Fomento de Construcciones
y Contratas (FCC)

Photos
  Fotos
Jordi Bernardó

Located in a dormitory suburb outside Barcelona, the development consists of 86 units of a single plan type, with buildings loosely arranged around the perimeter of a block with a central garden. The garden is planted with black poplars, and is accessible from the adjacent streets, joining a neighborhood network of pedestrian paths. The garden establishes a ground level for the housing units. Garage entries and commercial spaces are located below this level, opening to the surrounding streets as they descend in elevation.

Each 90 m² four-bedroom unit follows national standards for government-subsidized owner-occupied housing. Units open on two opposite exposures for through ventilation, with two units to each stair landing. Living-dining areas overlook both garden and street, and ground floor apartments have walled patios facing the garden.

The floor-to-ceiling windows and balconies vary only in their horizontal distribution from floor to floor, vibrating slightly within the strict order of the plans. While the proportions of the openings and street-line distribution of the buildings evoke 19th century urban typologies, the trim profiles and neat brickwork recall garden-suburb housing prototypes of the 1950s.

In einer Schlafstadt außerhalb Barcelonas gelegen, besteht dieser Komplex aus 86 Wohneinheiten mit einheitlichem Grundriß, wobei sich die einzelnen Baukörper locker um den Rand eines Blocks verteilen, in dessen Mitte ein Gartenhof liegt. Der Hof ist mit Schwarzpappeln bepflanzt, ist von der angrenzenden Straße zugänglich und wird somit Teil des Netzes von Fußgängerwegen im Viertel. Der Garten bildet das Erdgeschoßniveau für die Wohneinheiten. Garagenzufahrten und Gewerbeflächen liegen unterhalb dieses Niveaus und öffnen sich mit abnehmender Höhe zu den umliegenden Straßen.

Jede der 90 m² großen Einheiten mit fünf Zimmern entspricht den nationalen Standards für staatlich subventionierte Eigentumswohnungen. Die Einheiten sind an zwei gegenüberliegenden Seiten für die Durchlüftung geöffnet, wobei immer zwei Wohnungen an einen Treppenaufgang angeschlossen sind. Wohn- und Eßzimmer überblicken Garten und Straße. Die Parterrewohnungen haben zum Garten hin ummauerte Patios.

Die raumhohen Fenster und Balkone weichen von Geschoß zu Geschoß nur in ihrer horizontalen Anordnung leicht voneinander ab, ein auflockernder Akzent in der sonst strengen Ordnung. Während die Proportionen der Öffnungen und die

Central garden
Zentraler Grünbereich

Street elevation
Straßenfassade

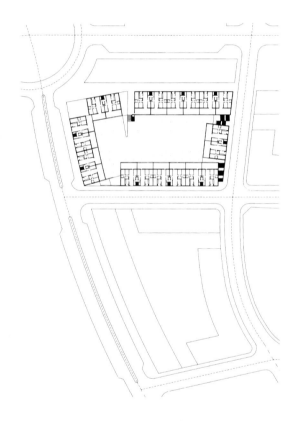

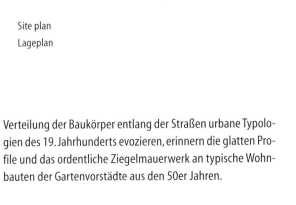

Site plan
Lageplan

Verteilung der Baukörper entlang der Straßen urbane Typologien des 19. Jahrhunderts evozieren, erinnern die glatten Profile und das ordentliche Ziegelmauerwerk an typische Wohnbauten der Gartenvorstädte aus den 50er Jahren.

Typical building plan
Regelgrundriß

Public Library – Torres Amat Factory Restoration   Sallent (Barcelona), 1989–1997
Öffentliche Bibliothek – Umbau der Torres Amat-Fabrik

Entry facade
Stair hall

Eingangsfassade
Treppenhalle

Client
  Auftraggeber
Architectural Patrimony Service,
City of Barcelona

Collaborator
  Mitarbeiter
Luis Maldonado

Technical architects
  Ausführungsplanung
Jaume Bassas, Antoni Elizondo

Builder
  Generalunternehmer
URCOTEX

Photos
  Fotos
Jordi Bernardó, M. Baldom

The public library for this small town on the Llobregat River has been installed in the 19th century wing of a historic textile factory. Other parts of the complex, including a water mill dating to the 17th century, will be restored as a museum. The library occupies the two upper floors of the wing, and is accessed via a new independent entry and vertical circulation system that has been inserted in one of its three bays. A wide wood stair rises to the first floor reading room,

Die öffentliche Bücherei für diese kleine Stadt am Llobregat wurde in dem aus dem 19. Jahrhundert stammenden Teil einer historischen Textilfabrik eingerichtet. Andere Teile des Komplexes, darunter eine Wassermühle, die auf das 17. Jahrhundert zurückgeht, werden als Museum restauriert. Die Bibliothek nimmt zwei Obergeschosse ein und ist über einen neuen unabhängigen Eingang und ein vertikales Erschließungssystem zugänglich, das in einer der drei Gewölbeschiffe

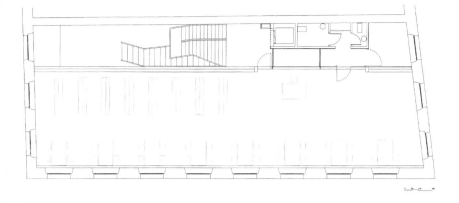

2nd floor plan, library
Grundriß zweites Geschoß,
Bibliothek

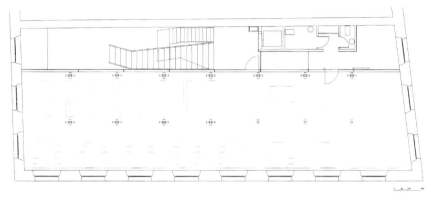

1st floor plan, library
Grundriß erstes Geschoß,
Bibliothek

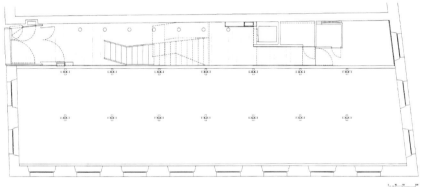

Entry level plan (new mezzanine
above ground floor)
Grundriß Eingangsgeschoß
(neues Halbgeschoß über Erdgeschoß)

while the second floor, which houses the museum archives, is reached via a narrower and steeper run of stairs, indicating its more restricted accessibility.

The existing structure of ceramic vaults resting on wood beams and cast iron columns was reinforced with a system of metal profiles, while the wood roof trusses were restored and fireproofed. The reading room windows are divided between an upper section, set flush with the stone exterior walls to capture light, and a lower operable section for ventilation, which is recessed in an oxidized and varnished steel frame so as to be within the reach of interior users. The architects refrained from further defining the spaces so as to allow their uses to be changed over time.

des Gebäudes untergebracht ist. Eine breite Holztreppe führt zum Lesesaal im ersten Stock, während das zweite Geschoß, in dem das Museumsarchiv liegt, über eine engere und steilere Treppe erreicht wird, Zeichen einer begrenzteren Zugänglichkeit.

Die bestehende Konstruktion von keramikverkleideten Gewölben, die auf Holzbalken und schmiedeeisernen Säulen ruhen, wurde durch ein System von Metallprofilen verstärkt, während die hölzernen Dachbalken restauriert und feuerfest gemacht wurden. Die Fenster des Lesesaals bestehen aus einem Oberteil, das direkt an die steinernen Außenmauern stößt, um möglichst viel Licht hereinzulassen, und einem Unterteil, das sich zur Belüftung öffnen läßt und das einen zurückgesetzten Rahmen aus passiviertem und lackiertem Stahl hat, so daß es für die Nutzer leicht erreichbar ist. Die Architekten verzichteten auf eine weitergehende Unterteilung der Räume, um unterschiedliche Nutzungen zuzulassen.

Rafael Aranda, Carme Pigem & Ramón Vilalta   Olot

The designs of Aranda, Pigem and Vilalta are produced from two principal lines of conceptual development: they are a response to the study and interpretation of a specific site and place; and they are carefully cultivated as abstract formal objects. These conceptual axes reflect the early fine arts training of Pigem and Vilalta. They result in buildings that are original and intriguingly aloof, and which often come into focus around intimate visual effects.

The three architects prefer to live and work in the country (Olot is a town of 28,000 inhabitants, not far from Girona). They defend the decision to cultivate their discipline far from the influences and rivalries of Barcelona colleagues, contending that it is now possible to maintain a vital, independent practice in a de-centralized, non-urban context. They maintain a non-hierarchical relation among themselves, working together around a single large table.

The group attracted early attention with the 1989 Punta Aldea Lighthouse in the Canary Islands. Their design broke with the conventional lighthouse typology of the tower, introducing a horizontal tapering form that is cantilevered from a rocky outcrop. The structure led to a French television documentary and an exhibition and commission in Japan. Their practice has evolved from far-flung competition-winning projects to local commissions such as the Law School for the University of Girona, set to open in the fall of 1999.

Aranda, Pigem und Vilalta entwickeln ihre Entwürfe aus zwei konzeptionellen Grundzügen: Sie entstehen aus dem Studium und der Interpretation der spezifischen Lage und des Ortes; und sie werden sorgsam als abstrakte formale Objekte herausgearbeitet. Diese konzeptionellen Axiome spiegeln die frühe künstlerische Ausbildung von Pigem und Vilalta. Sie führen zu Gebäuden, die ebenso originär wie faszinierend entrückt sind und häufig um intime visuelle Effekte zentriert sind.

Die drei Architekten ziehen es vor, auf dem Land zu leben und zu arbeiten (Olot ist ein kleines Städtchen von 28.000 Einwohnern unweit von Girona) und verteidigen ihre Entscheidung, ihre Profession weit entfernt von den Einflüssen und Rivalitäten ihrer Kollegen in Barcelona auszuüben. Ihrer Meinung nach ist es heute möglich, eine lebendige, unabhängige Praxis in einem dezentralen, nicht-städtischen Kontext aufrechtzuerhalten. Sie verzichten auf eine Rangordnung in ihrer Firma und arbeiten alle an einem gemeinsamen großen Tisch.

Die Gruppe erregte 1989 mit ihrem Punta Aldea-Leuchtturm auf den Kanarischen Inseln Aufsehen. Ihr Entwurf brach mit der konventionellen Leuchtturmtypologie, indem er eine horizontale, sich verjüngende Form schuf, die über felsigem Grund auskragt. Die Konstruktion regte einen französischen Dokumentarfilm an und führte zu einer Ausstellung und einem Auftrag aus Japan. Ihre Arbeit entwickelte sich von verschiedenen Wettbewerbsgewinnen hin zu lokalen Aufträgen wie der Juristischen Fakultät der Universität von Girona, die im Herbst 1999 eröffnet wird.

Access Pavilion, Fageda de Jordà Park   Santa Pau (Girona), 1994
Eingangspavillon, Fageda de Jordà Park

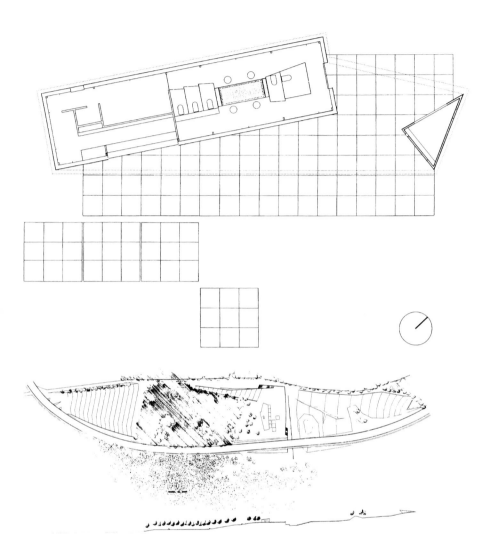

Pavilion floor plan

Grundriß des Pavillons

Site plan and sections
pavilion in center

Lageplan und Schnitt
mit Pavillon in der Mitte

The Fageda de Jordà is a large forest that has grown over a labyrinthine volcanic landscape scattered with small ash cones, lava spills and other topographic accidents. The pavilion is part of an otherwise unexecuted plan to introduce visitors to the park. It contains bar service and information windows (closed in photo), and restrooms. Its tubular steel structural frame supports a base of oxidized steel, walls of compressed wood fiberboard, and a copper roof. The restrooms are illuminated and ventilated from a central void, one of several measures that protect the structure from possible vandalism. The paving is of concrete finished to resemble basalt. The materials blend with the colors of the forest and the ground, while the twisted forms and projecting cornice give the small structure a large-scale presence.

Fageda de Jordà ist ein großes Waldgebiet, das in einer labyrinthhaften, mit verstreuten kleinen Aschekegeln, Lavagestein und anderen topografischen Unebenheiten übersäten Vulkanlandschaft entstand. Der Pavillon ist der einzige verwirklichte Teil eines Plans, den Park attraktiver zu machen. Er hat eine Bar, Informationsschaufenster mit Fotos sowie Toiletten. Seine röhrenförmige Stahlkonstruktion trägt einen Sockel aus oxydiertem Stahl, Wände aus Preßholzfaserplatten und ein Kupferdach. Die Toiletten erhalten Licht und Belüftung durch eine zentrale Öffnung, eine von mehreren Maßnahmen, um das Gebäude vor möglichem Vandalismus zu schützen. Der Boden besteht aus Beton, der so behandelt ist, daß er Basalt ähnelt. Die Materialien verschmelzen farblich mit dem Wald und dem Erdboden. Die gewundenen Formen und das vorspringende Gesims verleihen dem kleinen Gebäude eine beeindruckende Präsenz.

Client
 Auftraggeber
Department of Environment, Generalitat of Catalunya

Collaborators
 Mitarbeiter
M. Tàpies, A. Sàenz

Structural engineer
 Tragwerk
A. Blàzquez – L. Guanter

Photos
 Fotos
Eugeni Pons

Main facade
Hauptfassade

Bathroom
Toiletten

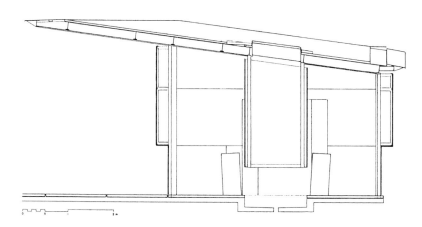

Section
Schnitt

Margarida House   Olot (Girona), 1994
Haus Margarida

Main facade
Upper corridor

Hauptfassade
Oberer Korridor

Main facade
Upper corridor

Hauptfassade
Oberer Korridor

Client
  Auftraggeber
Manuel Lagares &
Margarida Vilalta

Collaborator
  Mitarbeiter
M. Tàpies

Structural engineer
  Statik
A. Sàenz, R. Brufau, L. Moya

Photos
  Fotos
Eugeni Pons

A simple design produces a rich combination of indoor/out-door spaces. The T-shaped plan comprises a long two-story volume intersected at its center by the one-story kitchen. The kitchen divides the entry zone from the garden, which is located at a higher level following the slope of the terrain, and which includes a small lap pool set directly against the lot wall facing the street. The two-story band of windows of the garden facade is interrupted by a suspended canopy of horizontal glass, with wood slats spanning between the light steel trusses beneath it. The canopy shades the ground floor while reflecting light into the studio above it.

The outdoor zone defined by the canopy is finished in wood flooring, and the ground floor windows can be slid away, extending living areas into the garden. Adjustable lou-vers provide optional sun protection. Inside, the stair rises beside a double-height space, which is crossed by a balcony that separates the upstairs studio from the bedroom zone. The main bedroom is located on the ground floor opposite the entry. A terrace above the kitchen volume affords views over the neighborhood.

Ein schlichter Entwurf schafft hier eine reiche Kombination von Innen- und Außenräumen. Der T-förmige Grundriß um-faßt einen langen zweigeschossigen Baukörper, der in seinem Zentrum von der eingeschossigen Küche unterbrochen wird. Die Küche teilt den Eingangsbereich vom Garten ab, der, dem ansteigenden Terrain folgend, auf einem höheren Niveau liegt und direkt an der Grundstücksmauer zur Straße ein kleines Schwimmbecken hat. Das zweigeschossige Fensterband der Gartenfassade ist von einem schwebenden gläsernen Vordach unterbrochen, getragen von Holzleisten, die von leichten Stahl-trägern gestützt werden. Das Vordach beschattet das Erdge-schoß, während er in das Studio darüber Licht reflektiert. Der Außenraum, den das Vordach definiert, ist mit einem Holzbo-den versehen, und die Verglasungen des Erdgeschosses lassen sich beiseite schieben, um den Wohnbereich in den Garten auszudehnen. Verstellbare Fensterläden bieten bei Bedarf zu-sätzlichen Schutz vor der Sonne.

Innen steigt die Treppe an der Seite eines zweigeschossigen Raumes nach oben. Ein Balkon durchkreuzt diesen Raum und trennt das Studio im Obergeschoß vom Bereich der Schlafzim-mer darunter. Das Hauptschlafzimmer liegt im Erdgeschoß gegenüber dem Eingang. Die Terrasse über dem Küchentrakt bietet Ausblicke über die Umgebung.

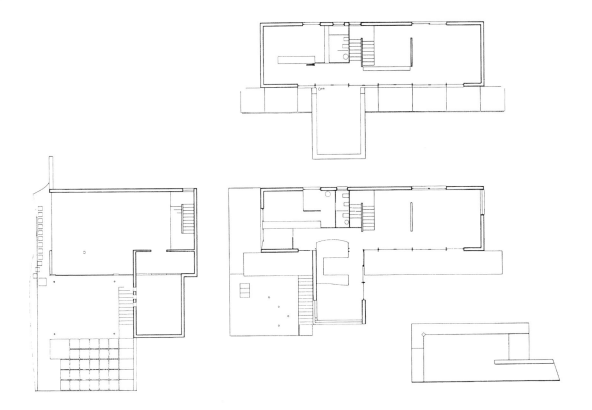

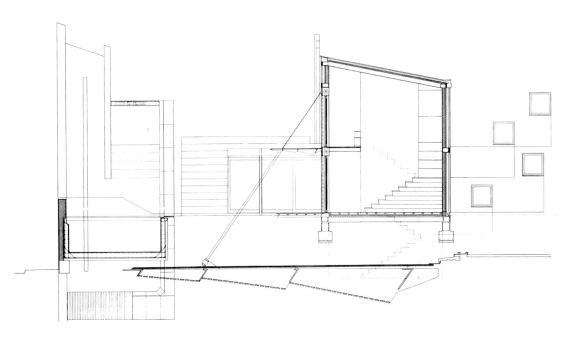

View into stair hall, living room
Blick in das Wohnzimmer mit Treppenaufgang

Upper level, main facade with glass canopy
Obergeschoß, Hauptfassade mit Glasvordach

Upper floor plan (top), ground floor plan (center right), semi-basement plan (center left)
Grundriß Obergeschoß (oben); Mitte rechts: Grundriß Erdgeschoß; Mitte links: Grundriß Souterrain

Details (bottom)
Details (unten)

Law School, University of Girona   Montilivi Campus, Girona, 1995–2000
Juristische Fakultät der Universität Girona

Entry elevation
Eingangsfassade

The campus master plan (by others) was rather insensitively divided into flat square building blocks over a steeply-sloping terrain. The architects resolve the ten-meter slope across the site with a three-story building that is largely underground. Only an upper floor of horizontal volumes, monolithically clad in limestone and white glass, projects sculpturally over sloping limestone berms.

In plan, parallel rows of light trenches alternate with built volumes, and are crossed by perpendicular circulation spines. The building is accessed from a street-level plaza on its southwest border. The high volume of the main auditorium beside the entry anchors the design from the exterior. Beside it, a three-story hall on the lowest floor provides an interior focus. It gathers public spaces such as the cafeteria and copy center, as well as secondary exits through the earth berms to the street and tunnels to other buildings.

The rows of classroom volumes terminate in professors' offices, which are arranged around three small light courts.

Der Masterplan des Campus – der von anderen Architekten stammt – sah weitgehend eine Bebauung des steil abschüssigen Geländes mit flachen, rechteckigen Blocks vor. Die Architekten reagieren auf den zehn Meter langen Hang des Grundstücks mit einem dreigeschossigen Gebäude, das weitgehend unter der Erde liegt. Nur ein Obergeschoß aus liegenden Baukörpern, das monolithisch mit Kalkstein und weißem Glas verkleidet ist, erhebt sich skulptural über den mit Kalkstein verkleideten Böschungen.

Im Grundriß alternieren mit den Körpern parallele, lichterfüllte Einschnitte, die sich mit Erschließungsachsen kreuzen. Das Gebäude ist von dem Vorplatz auf Straßenniveau an der Südwestecke des Grundstückes zugänglich. Das hohe Volumen des Hauptauditoriums neben dem Eingang bildet den äußeren Fokus des Komplexes, eine Funktion, die im Inneren eine vom untersten Niveau dreigeschossig aufstrebende Halle übernimmt. Hier bündeln sich öffentliche Räume wie die Cafeteria und das Kopierzentrum ebenso wie Nebenausgänge zur

Client
  Auftraggeber
University of Girona

Collaborators
  Mitarbeiter
A. Sàenz, M. Tàpies, F. Wien

Technical architect
  Ausführungsplanung
P. Rif

Structural engineer
  Tragwerk
A. Blàzquez – L. Guanter

Mechanical engineer
  Haustechnik
J. Viñas

Photos
  Fotos
Eugeni Pons

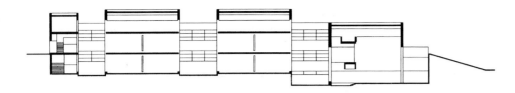

Section at interior hall
Schnitt durch die Innenhalle

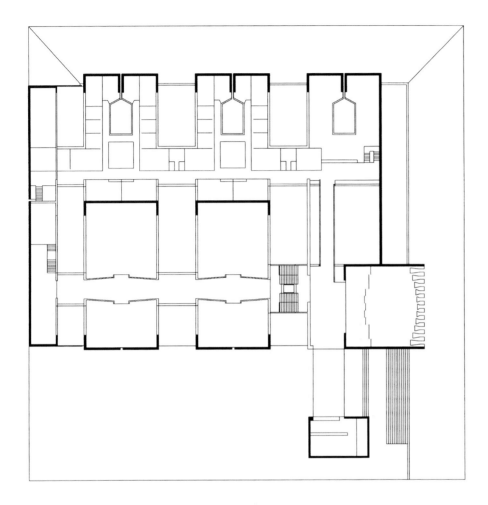

Entry level floor plan
Grundriß Eingangsgeschoß

The design includes interesting details such as the horizontal band of white glass that elevates the top-story volumes over the sloping berms; the auditorium facade, a ridged grille of white glass; and the sunken central interior space, crisscrossed by bridges and overlooking a light well.

Straße und Tunnelübergänge zu anderen Gebäuden. Die Reihen der Seminartrakte leiten über zu den Büros der Professoren, die um drei kleine Lichthöfe gruppiert sind.

Zur Gestaltung gehören interessante Details wie das horizontale Band aus weißem Glas, mit dem sich die Körper des Obergeschosses über den Hang erheben; die Rippenfassade des Auditoriums aus weißem Glas; ein abgesenkter zentraler Innenraum mit Lichthof, der von Brücken gekreuzt wird.

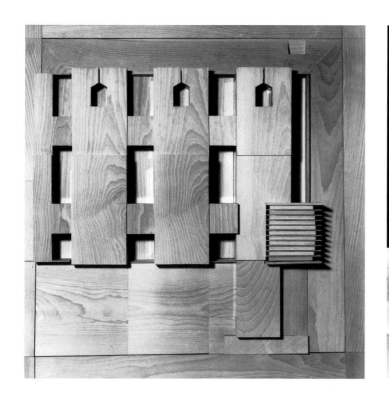

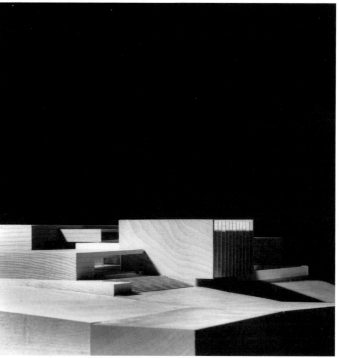

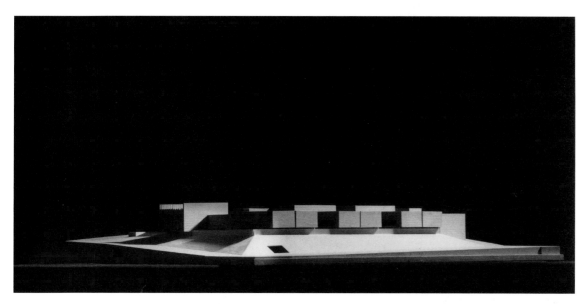

Model views
Modellansichten

Francisco Mangado Pamplona

As an influential teacher and critic, prolific designer, and active presence on the national scene, Francisco "Patxi" Mangado is a key point of reference for architecture in northern Spain. With contemporaries such as Roberto Ercilla and Eduardo de Miguel, he has helped open the School of Architecture in Pamplona to contemporary design currents, including a pioneering teaching program of visiting national and international figures.

Mangado is an architect's architect, in the sense that he subjects the design problem to a rigorous intellectual scrutiny in which nothing is taken for granted. He advocates a spirit of creative investigation unsupported by "apriori credos" or conventions, in a "naked confrontation" with the design problem which he compares to the art of bullfighting.

The resulting work may seem at first difficult to engage, as it offers few familiar points of stylistic reference, but it stands very solidly on its own formal premises. Mangado attracted early attention for projects such as the 1987 Plaza Carlos III in Olite and the 1990 Marcus Real Winery, but he considers of greater formative importance his 1991 studies for an unbuilt hotel in Pamplona, and the 1994 competition for the Castilla-León Concert Hall. He is currently working on two major works, the Navarra Congress Hall, winner of an open competition, and a monastery in Goa, India.

Als einflußreicher Lehrer und Kritiker und als produktiver und engagierter Entwerfer ist Francisco „Patxi" Mangado eine Schlüsselgestalt der nordspanischen Architekturszene. Zusammen mit Zeitgenossen wie Roberto Ercilla und Eduardo de Miguel leistete er einen Beitrag, um die Architekturfakultät Pamplona für aktuelle Strömungen zu öffnen, unter anderem mit einer neuen Vorlesungsreihe mit Gastdozenten aus dem In- und Ausland.

Mangado ist ein klassischer Architekt in dem Sinne, daß er das Gestaltungsproblem einer strengen intellektuellen Analyse unterzieht, in der nichts als selbstverständlich vorausgesetzt wird. Er vertritt einen Geist kreativer Forschung, der sich nicht auf a priori feststehende „Glaubenssätze" oder Konventionen stützt und statt dessen eine „nackte Konfrontation" mit dem Gestaltungsproblem sucht, die er mit der Kunst des Stierkampfs vergleicht.

Die sich daraus ergebende Arbeit mag zunächst schwer zugänglich erscheinen, da sie wenige vertraute stilistische Bezugspunkte bietet, aber sie ist in ihren eigenen formalen Prämissen fest verankert. Mangado erregte frühe Aufmerksamkeit mit Projekten wie der Plaza Carlos III in Olite von 1987 und der Weinkellerei Marcus Real von 1990, aber für ihn selbst haben seine Studien für ein nicht realisiertes Hotel in Pamplona von 1991 und sein Beitrag zum Wettbewerb für die Castilla-León-Konzerthalle einen höheren Stellenwert für seinen beruflichen Werdegang. Gegenwärtig arbeitet er an zwei großen Projekten: der Navarra-Kongreßhalle, mit deren Entwurf er den offenen Wettbewerb gewann, und ein Kloster in Goa in Indien.

Zuasti Country Club   Señorio de Zuasti (Navarra), 1992–1998
Zuasti Country Club

Bar pavilion, left; dressing rooms, right

Links: Barpavillon; rechts: Umkleideräume

Mangado was asked to convert a large, early-century estate outside Pamplona into an American-style golf and country club. His master plan foresees an incremental introduction of new elements to the grounds over time, including the conversion of the original mansion into a clubhouse, now underway.

The facilities built to date are organized along a spine linking the entry gate to the original house. Mangado has graded the sloping terrain into a series of terraces, allowing the cafeteria and indoor pool to be semi-buried under the upper terrace, with porches opening to a lower terrace. Two discrete pavilions, one containing the bar and the other dressing rooms and a top-floor exercise room, are intuitively sited astride the upper terrace in response to the landscape and views, assuming a role similar to that of the estate's former agricultural dependencies.

Mangado's intention is to create an inhabited, ludic landscape or garden, suggestively open to "mutable, often im-

Mangado wurde beauftragt, ein großes Anwesen außerhalb von Pamplona vom Beginn des Jahrhunderts in einen Golf- und Country Club amerikanischen Stils zu verwandeln. Sein Masterplan sieht vor, daß über die Zeit neue Elemente hinzugefügt werden können, darunter die Umwandlung des ursprünglichen Herrenhauses in ein Clubhaus, die gegenwärtig vorgenommen wird.

Die bis heute gebauten Einrichtungen gliedern sich entlang einer Achse, die das Eingangstor mit dem Herrensitz verbindet. Mangado hat das abschüssige Terrain in eine Reihe von Terrassen gestuft, so daß die Cafeteria und das Schwimmbecken halb unter der oberen Terrasse liegen, mit Portalen, die sich zu einer tieferen Terrasse öffnen. Zwei einzeln stehende Pavillons, von denen einer die Bar und der andere Umkleideräume und einen Übungsraum im Obergeschoß enthält, sind in Reaktion auf die Landschaft und Ausblicke intuitiv zu beiden Seiten der oberen Terrasse gesetzt, wo sie die Rolle übernehmen, die zuvor die ehemaligen Nebengebäude des Anwesens innehatten.

Client
Auftraggeber
Señorio de Zuasti, S.A.

Collaborators
Mitarbeiter
MRA Technical Services

Photos
Fotos
César San Millán

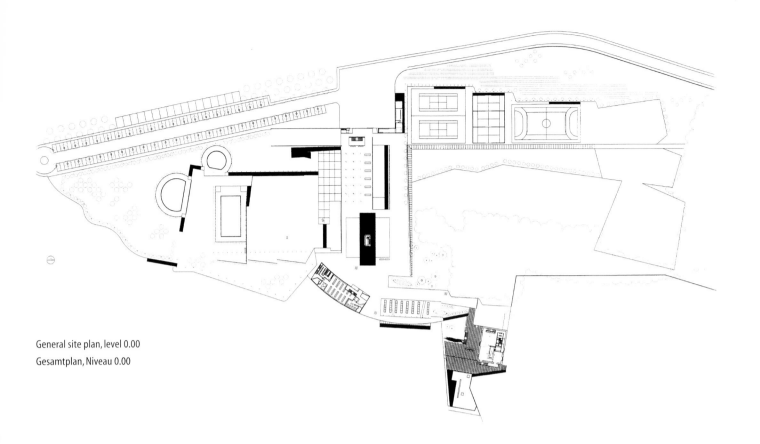

General site plan, level 0.00

Gesamtplan, Niveau 0.00

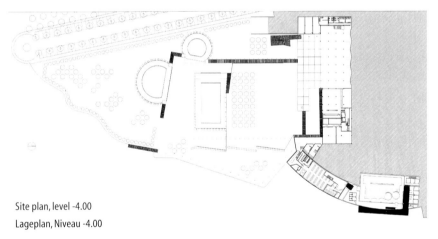

Site plan, level -4.00

Lageplan, Niveau -4.00

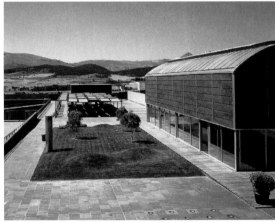

View from dressing rooms
towards entry

Blick von den Umkleideräumen
zum Eingang

Original house; indoor pool terrace, left

Ursprüngliches Herrenhaus; links: Terrasse am Schwimmbecken

Entry facade, dressing rooms

Eingangsfassade, Umkleideräume

East-west section through cafeteria

Ost-West-Schnitt durch die Cafeteria

North-south section through indoor pool

Nord-Süd-Schnitt durch das Innenschwimmbecken

provised uses" through the generous provision of "formally specific but unprogrammed intermediate spaces." In this spirit, the two freestanding pavilions are conceived much like pieces of furniture: lightweight, almost moveable in appearance, simple in composition, and finely finished in clapboards of tropical wood. At night, the upper terrace is suggestively defined by a continuous low glass wall between the entry and bar, which provides the principal site lighting.

Mangados Absicht war es, eine bewohnte, spielerische Landschaft oder einen Garten zu schaffen, der durch die großzügige Gestaltung „formal spezifischer, jedoch nicht programmatisch festgelegter Zwischenräume" anregend offen für „veränderbare, häufig improvisierte Nutzungen" ist. In diesem Geist sind die beiden freistehenden Pavillons ganz ähnlich wie Möbelstücke konzipiert: leichtgewichtig, in ihrer Erscheinung beinahe beweglich, schlicht in der Komposition und mit Edelholz gediegen verkleidet. Nachts wird die obere Terrasse suggestiv von einer durchlaufenden, niedrigen Glaswand zwischen dem Eingang und der Bar definiert, die auch für die Beleuchtung des Grundstücks sorgt.

Subsidized Housing Cizur Mayor   Pamplona, 1996–1998
Geförderter Wohnkomplex Cizur Mayor

Patio with detail of exterior
finishes

Patio with street facade

Patio mit Detail der Außenfassade

Patio mit Straßenfassade

Client
  Auftraggeber
Miguel Rico & Associates

Collaborators
  Mitarbeiter
Carlos Peredes, Mikel Sáenz

Photos
  Fotos
César San Millán

Shown is the first of two symmetrically identical housing blocks, one privately sponsored, the other a public promotion, and both conforming to the standards and budgets of subsidized housing. Mangado opened three corners of the original master plan's closed patio-block volume, creating two longitudinal buildings and an L-shaped volume around a central garden. Bedrooms overlook the hard street facades, through small, regularly-spaced windows, while the living areas, kitchen and common entries overlook the more domestic common garden, with its more open and harmoniously composed facades. The through-block unit plans offer a certain flexibility of layout within a standard three-bedroom, two-bath format. Ground floor units are compensated with small private yards.

The formal identity of the design is established mainly through the articulation of the window openings. The horizontal lines of the garden facade windows are reinforced by panels of veneered marine plywood, while the punched-out quality of the street fenestration is underscored by the painted metal finishes that line the deep wall cut-outs. The open corner overlooking a small traffic circle is articulated as a diagonal cut in the building block. Its angled walls are sheathed in fiber cement board panels, interrupting the continuity of the facade's stucco-finished masonry.

Gezeigt wird der erste von zwei symmetrisch identischen Häuserblöcken, von denen der eine privat finanziert, der andere öffentlich gefördert wird, beide gemäß den Standards und Budgets des staatlich subventionierten Wohnungsbaus. Mangado öffnete drei Ecken des geschlossenen, patioartigen Blockvolumens, das der ursprüngliche Masterplan vorsah, indem er zwei Längsgebäude und einen L-förmigen Baukörper um eine zentrale Grünanlage schuf. Die Zimmer sind zu den strengen Straßenfassaden hin ausgerichtet, während der Wohnbereich, die Küche und die Eingänge auf den häuslichen Gemeinschaftsgarten mit seinen offeneren und harmonisch gestalteten Fassaden blicken. Die Grundrisse des Durchgangsblocks bieten eine gewisse Flexibilität innerhalb des Standards von vier Zimmern und zwei Bädern. Die Wohneinheiten im Erdgeschoß haben zum Ausgleich kleine private Höfe.

Die formale Identität der Gestaltung wird hauptsächlich durch die Artikulation der Fensteröffnungen hergestellt. Die horizontalen Linien der Fenster der Gartenfassaden werden von Furnierpaneelen betont, während die wie ausgestanzt wirkenden Fenster zur Straße von den lackierten Metallverblendungen hervorgehoben werden, die die tiefen Laibungen verkleiden. Die offene Ecke, die einen kleinen Kreisverkehr überblickt, bildet einen diagonalen Einschnitt in den Gebäudeblock. Ihre beiden schräg zulaufenden Wände sind mit Zementfaserplatten verkleidet, die die Kontinuität der verputzten Mauerwerksfassaden unterbrechen.

90

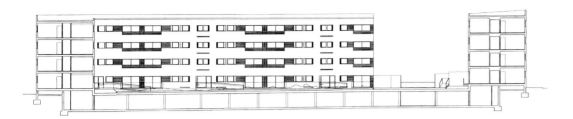

Section elevation

Schnittansicht

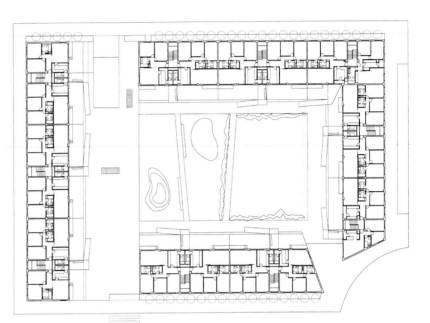

Detail, chamfered corner, entries

Teilansicht der offenen Gebäude-
ecke, Eingänge

Plan, floors 1, 2, 3

Grundriß erstes, zweites und
drittes Geschoß

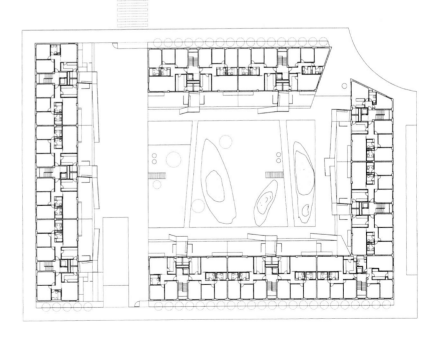

91

Gamesa Eólica Factory   Pamplona, 1996–1997
Gamesa Eólica-Fabrik

Client
Auftraggeber
Gamesa Eólica S.A

Collaborators
Mitarbeiter
Juan Catalán, Mikel Sáenz

Project manager
Projektleiter
Iturralde & Sagues, Engineers

Photos
Fotos
César San Millán

For a factory producing wind-driven electric power turbines, Mangado combines three production bays and offices in a single volume, using the contrasting scales of the program elements to create formal tension and dialogue. The office section is organized around an interior light court and garden, and a diaphanous backlit stair. Ground floor employee dressing rooms and production control offices are succeeded by second floor administrative offices and a third floor conference room, whose large glass window directs views over the industrial surroundings to a distant line of hills, where a row of the company's turbines can be seen. The substantial mechanical services are located in a triangular space behind the office section.

The factory exterior is clad in an inexpensive corrugated steel sheet, normally used for roof decking, with wood bumpers at its base, while the offices are clad in conventional metal panels of the same finish. The formal dialogue between offices and factory occurs around the common horizontal line that marks the top of this taut metal skin. A horizontal band of translucent glass at the top of the production shed walls, marking the zone of sawtooth skylights and trusses, establishes a firm visual counterweight to the dynamic, angular gesture of the conference room volume towards the mountains.

Bei diesem Fabrikgebäude für eine Firma, die Turbinen für die Gewinnung von Windenergie herstellt, kombinierte Mangado drei Produktionsabteilungen und Büros in einem einzigen Volumen, indem er die kontrastierenden Dimensionen der Programmelemente einsetzte, um Spannung und Dialog zu schaffen. Der Bürobereich ist um einen Lichthof mit Garten und ein transluzentes, von hinten beleuchtetes Treppenhaus organisiert. Den Personalräumen der Beschäftigten im Erdgeschoß und den Büros der Produktionskontrolle folgen im zweiten Geschoß Verwaltungsbüros und im dritten ein Konferenzraum, dessen großes Glasfenster Ausblicke über das umliegende Industriegebiet und eine entfernte Hügelkette bietet, wo einige Windräder der Firma zu besichtigen sind. Die umfängliche Haustechnik ist in einem dreieckigen Raum hinter dem Bürobereich untergebracht.

Außen ist die Fabrik mit einem kostengünstigen Wellblech verkleidet, das sonst für Dächer benutzt wird und hier am Sockel mit Holzkanten abschließt, während die Bürofassaden aus konventionellen Metallpaneelen der gleichen Art bestehen. Der formale Dialog zwischen Büros und Fabrik entsteht um die gemeinsame horizontale Linie, die die Spitze dieser straffen Metallhaut markiert. Ein horizontales Band aus transluzentem Glas, das den oberen Abschluß der Produktionshalle bildet und den Bereich der Oberlichter des Sheddaches und der oberen Träger markiert, schafft ein festes visuelles Gegengewicht zur dynamischen Geste des kantigen Volumens des Konferenzraumes, das auf die Berge blickt.

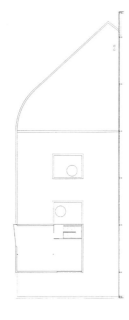

First floor plan
Grundriß 1. Obergeschoß

Second floor plan
Grundriß 2. Obergeschoß

Southwest facade with top floor projecting conference room
Südwestansicht mit dem auskragenden Konferenzraum im Obergeschoß

Southeast facade at entry
Südostansicht mit Eingang

Southwest facade
Südwestansicht

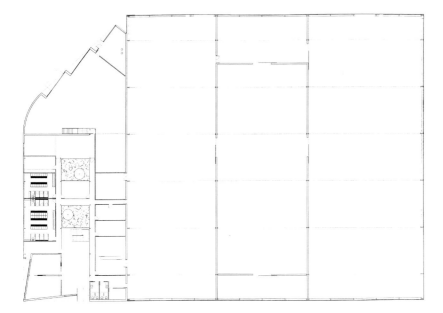

Ground floor plan
Grundriß Erdgeschoß

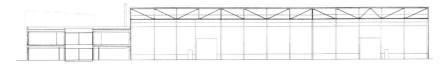

Section
Schnitt

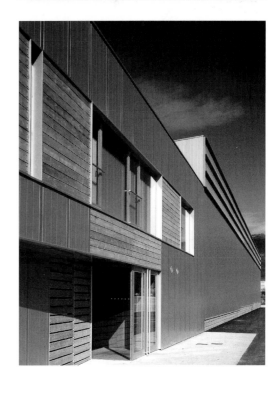

Fernando Tabuenca & Jesús Leache Pamplona
Eduardo de Miguel Valencia

Eduardo de Miguel completed two important projects in Pamplona with Jesús Leache, the Azpilagaña Medical Clinic and the Gráficas Lizarra Factory, before relocating to Valencia and establishing an independent practice. At roughly the same time, Fernando Tabuenca, a classmate and friend from the Navarra School of Architecture, returned to Pamplona from a period in the studio of Rafael Moneo, and began a new professional association with Leache with the Urroz-Villa Frontón. We thus present the work of two independent studios, whose intersecting trajectories have only recently taken separate paths.

The studios share a similar approach to design. Both advocate the rational analysis of program, setting and technical means as a working method over the use of preconceived styles or formalisms. And both give precedence to the role of architecture as a service to clients and users, which they oppose to its cultivation as a self-referential professional discourse. For Tabuenca and Leache, this philosophy has resulted so far in a more eclectic body of work, open to circumstance and experiment. De Miguel on the other hand appears to be working towards a more consistent formal development, in which circumstance is addressed and absorbed by the rational tools and codes of the modern tradition.

Eduardo de Miguel vollendete zusammen mit Jesús Leache zwei wichtige Projekte in Pamplona, die Medizinische Klinik Azpilagaña und die Fabrik Gráficas Lizarra, bevor er nach Valencia zurückging und dort sein eigenes Architekturbüro gründete. Ungefähr zur gleichen Zeit kehrte Fernando Tabuenca, ein Kommilitone und Freund aus der gemeinsamen Zeit an der Architekturschule von Navarra, nach Pamplona zurück, nachdem er eine Zeitlang im Büro von Rafael Moneo gearbeitet hatte, und begann mit dem Pelotaspielfeld (Frontón) in Urroz-Villa (Navarra) eine neue berufliche Zusammenarbeit mit Leache. So präsentieren wir hier die Arbeit von zwei unabhängigen Architekturbüros, deren berufliche Wege sich kreuzten und erst seit kurzem wieder in getrennte Richtungen führen.

Beide Studios teilen einen ähnlichen Gestaltungsansatz. Beide treten für eine rationale Analyse des Programms, der Lage und der technischen Mittel als Arbeitsmethode ein und sprechen sich gegen Formalismus und im vorhinein festgelegte Stile aus. Und beide verstehen Architektur in erster Linie als Dienst an den Kunden und Nutzern, nicht als Kultivierung eines selbstreferentiellen Architekturdiskurses. Für Tabuenca und Leache hat diese Philosophie bislang zu einem relativ hybriden Werk geführt, das offen für äußere Einflüsse und Experimente ist. De Miguel scheint auf der anderen Seite stärker nach einer konsequenten formalen Entwicklung zu streben, bei der die äußeren Umstände durch rationale Werkzeuge und Codes der modernen Tradition aufgegriffen und absorbiert werden.

Azpilagaña Medical Clinic   Pamplona, 1989–1993
Azpilagaña-Klinik

Street facade
Straßenfassade

Top floor at stair
Obergeschoß an der Treppe

Built by the regional government, this public outpatient center is part of a special program of commissions given to young architects, including Tabuenca's Medical Clinic in Olite and Francisco Mangado's in the Iturrama section of Pamplona. The building is focused inward in response to a restricted site surrounded by tall residential buildings. The windows of the examining rooms overlook a closed light court, assuring privacy and generous natural light. Waiting areas are naturally lit from a screened rear facade. The steep slope of the site permits a mid-level entry, with the three public levels no more than a single flight of stairs away. The tough finishes, including exposed brick walls in interior public areas, are softened by washes of diffused natural light from screened openings and clerestories.

Erbaut von der Regionalregierung, gehört diese Poliklinik zu einem besonderen Programm von Aufträgen an junge Architekten, worunter auch Tabuencas Klinik in Olite und Francisco Mangados Klinik im Iturrama-Bezirk von Pamplona fielen. In Reaktion auf das beengte Grundstück, das von hohen Wohngebäuden umgeben ist, kehrt sich das Gebäude nach innen. Die Fenster der Untersuchungsräume überblicken einen geschlossenen Lichthof, der Uneinsehbarkeit und einen großzügigen Lichteinfall gewährleistet. Warteräume werden durch die mit Sichtblenden versehene Rückfassade natürlich belichtet. Der steile Hang des Grundstücks ermöglichte die Schaffung eines Eingangs auf mittlerem Niveau, von dem die drei öffentlich zugänglichen Ebenen jeweils nicht weiter als eine Treppenflucht entfernt sind. Die rauhe Behandlung der Wände, darunter freiliegendes Mauerwerk im öffentlichen Bereich, wird durch diffuses Licht gemildert, das durch abgeschirmte Öffnungen und Lichtgaden einfällt.

Client
  Auftraggeber
Government of Navarra Health Service

Architects
  Architekten
De Miguel & Leache

Technical architect
  Ausführungsplanung
Jesús Ederra

Structural engineer
  Tragwerk
Miguel Ángel Zozaya

Mechanical engineer
  Haustechnik
Iturralde & Sagües

Builder
  Generalunternehmer
V.T.S

Photos
  Fotos
Luis Prieto, César San Millán

Entry hall, stair
Eingangshalle und Treppe

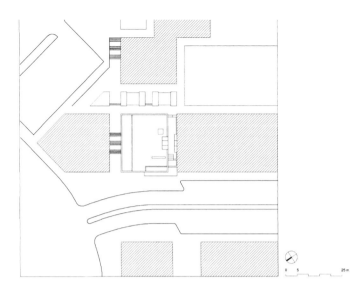

Site plan
Lageplan

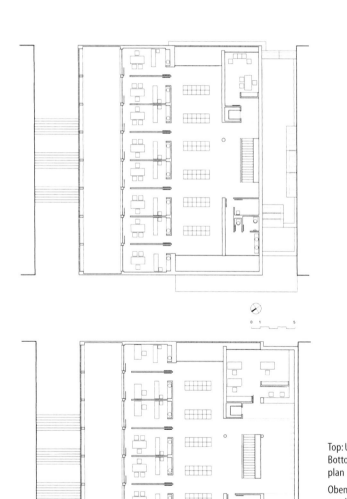

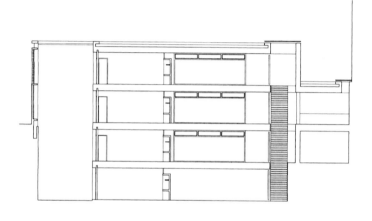

Top: Upper level plan
Bottom: Entry level
plan

Oben: Grundriß Ober-
geschoß
unten: Grundriß
Eingangsniveau

Sections
Schnitte

Frontón Urroz-Villa (Navarra), 1990–1991
Frontón-Stadion

Side elevation
Seitenfassade

Client
  Auftraggeber
Town of Urroz-Villa

Architects
  Architekten
Tabuenca & Leache

Structural engineer
  Tragwerk
Javier Errea

Builders
  Generalunternehmer
Jesús Labiano, masonry; Pedro
Ariz, metal structure; Wonder
Internacional, roof

Photos
  Fotos
Luis Prieto

This court for playing jai alai, a Basque sport, is located in the recreational park of a small rural town, beside a football field and a future swimming pool. Built on a tiny budget, it is composed of precast concrete walls and an arching roof of galvanized steel ribs alternating with transparent polyester seams. The self-supporting steel ribs, normally used in agricultural structures, are tensed into a semi-barrel vault. The roof is suspended tensely over the court, held in place by a complex assembly of steel channels, masts and cables. The architects compare its bold form to a sail; it also bears a certain resemblance to the hand-held wicker scoops used in the sport.

Das Stadion des squashähnlichen Pelotaspiels (jai alai) liegt im Erholungspark einer kleinen ländlichen Stadt neben einem Fußballplatz und einem künftigen Schwimmbad. Mit geringem Budget erbaut, besteht es aus vorgefertigten Betonmauern und einem gewölbten Dach aus verzinkten Stahlrippen mit transparenten Polyesterfugen. Die selbsttragenden Stahlrippen, die üblicherweise bei landwirtschaftlichen Bauten verwendet werden, spannen sich zu einem Tonnengewölbe. Das Dach ist straff über den Hof gespannt und mit einem komplexen Geflecht von Stahlsträngen, Masten und Kabeln verankert. Die Architekten vergleichen seine kühne Form mit einem Segel; es hat auch eine gewisse Ähnlichkeit mit den geflochtenen Fangschlägern, die beim Pelotaspiel verwendet werden.

Details of roof structure
Teilansichten der Dachkonstruktion

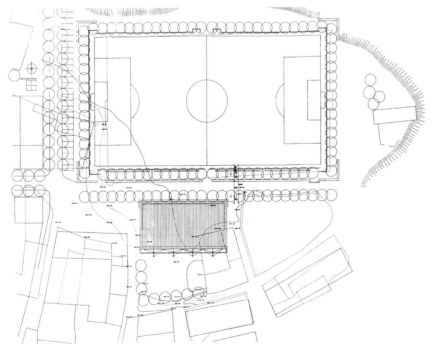

Layout plan
Lageplan

Temporary Public Housing   El Carmen, Valencia, 1994–1997
Übergangswohnungen

Typical unit interior
Typische Innengestaltung

Client
Auftraggeber
Regional government of Valencia

Architect
Architekt
Eduardo de Miguel

Collaborator
Mitarbeiter
Pascual Sellés

Builder
Generalunternehmer
Ortíz & Sons

Photos
Fotos
Miguel Ángel Valero

El Carmen is a historic but degraded neighborhood in the heart of the city. This eight-unit 550 m^2 structure supplies temporary housing to families displaced by public rehabilitation efforts. Built over the ruins of two existing structures, it combines local typologies with large modern openings, using load-bearing walls and floor slabs built up from prefab concrete joists and arched tiles.

Studio apartments of 32 m^2 and two-bedroom 50 m^2 units include ample crawl space above kitchens and baths for storing furniture and belongings. Living areas overlook a small plaza and an interior garden. To maintain a surviving street facade, the windows for one of the bedrooms overlook a void within the building shell, with oblique street views through diagonal cuts in a protruding corner. The exterior walls are painted white to maximize reflected luminosity in the extremely narrow street.

El Carmen ist ein heruntergekommenes Altstadtviertel im Herzen von Valencia. Dieses Gebäude mit acht Wohneinheiten von insgesamt 550 m^2 bietet Übergangswohnungen für Familien, die aufgrund der städtischen Sanierungsmaßnahmen Ersatzwohnraum benötigen. Über den Ruinen von zwei Altbauten errichtet, kombiniert es örtliche Typologien mit großen modernen Öffnungen. Die Mauern haben tragende Funktion und die Decken bestehen aus vorgefertigten Betonträgern und gewölbten Platten.

Zu den Studioapartments von 32 m^2 und Drei-Zimmer-Wohnungen von je 50 m^2 gehört ausgiebiger Stauraum über der Küche und dem Bad, um Möbel und andere Habe unterzubringen. Die Wohnzimmer überblicken einen kleinen Platz und einen Innengarten. Um eine alte Straßenfassade zu erhalten, blicken die Fenster eines der Schlafzimmer in einen Zwischenraum innerhalb der Gebäudehülle: Durch diagonale Schnitte in einer vorstehenden Ecke bieten sich hier schräge Ausblicke auf die Straße. Die Außenwände sind weiß gestrichen, um in der äußerst engen Straße die Reflexionswirkung zu maximieren.

Plaza elevation

Platzfassade

Roof terrace with views of
San Carlos church

Dachterrasse mit Ausblick auf die
Kirche San Carlos

Section from street to garden

Schnitt von der Straße zum
Garten

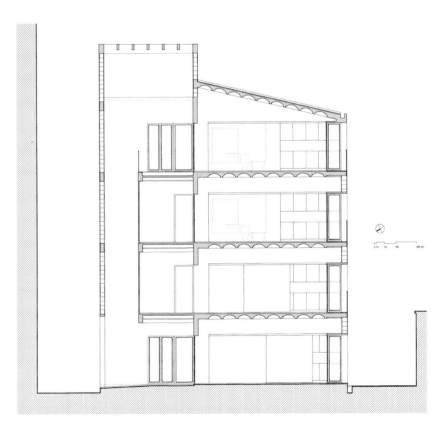

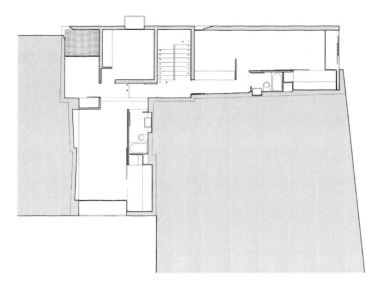

1st, 2nd floor plan

Grundriß erstes und zweites
Geschoß

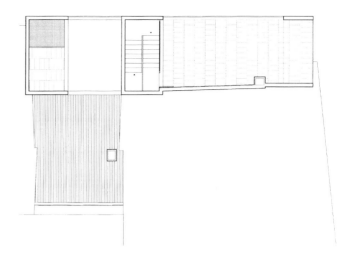

Roof plan

Grundriß Dachebene

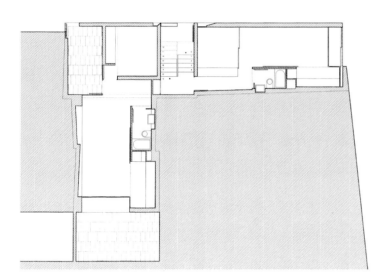

Ground floor plan

Grundriß Erdgeschoß

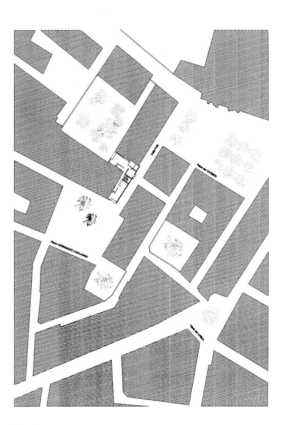

Site plan

Lageplan

Foral Police Station   Tudela (Navarra), 1996–
Foral Polizeiwache

Approach to main entry
Weg zum Haupteingang

The station is the first to be built for the regional autonomy's new police force. It commands a dramatic site atop a steep ravine, widely visible from the Pamplona-Zaragoza highway and the valley of the Ebro River. The design typologically resembles an aircraft carrier. Open-air vehicle parking, a detention area and corps lockers and meeting rooms are contained on two levels in the "hull," while offices for chief personnel are situated in a circular "watchtower" over the entry "deck" and heliport. The design is unmistakable as a contemporary vehicular-oriented police station. Its clean modern vocabulary is transparent to the client's values and concerns, from functional issues such as surveillance and security to the more subjective expression of strength, hierarchy, authority and control.

Die Wache ist die erste, die für die neuen Polizeikräfte der regionalen Autonomieverwaltung gebaut wird. Sie beherrscht eine dramatische Lage über einer steilen Schlucht und ist von der Autobahn Pamplona-Saragossa und dem Ebro-Tal weithin sichtbar. Die typologische Gestaltung erinnert an einen Flugzeugträger. Offene Parkplätze, ein Verwahrungsbereich, die Spinde der Polizeitruppe und Gemeinschaftsräume befinden sich auf zwei Ebenen im „Unterschiff", während die Büros für die Vorgesetzten in einem runden „Wachturm" über dem „Eingangsdeck" und dem Hubschrauberlandeplatz liegen. Die auf Fahrzeugverkehr zugeschnittene Gestaltung verweist unverkennbar auf eine moderne Polizeistation. An ihrem klaren modernen Vokabular lassen sich die Werte und Belange der Nutzer unmittelbar erkennen, von funktionalen Fragen wie der Überwachung und Sicherheit bis zu dem subjektiveren Eindruck von Stärke, Hierarchie, Autorität und Kontrolle.

Client
  Auftraggeber
Regional government of Navarra

Architects
  Architekten
Tabuenca & Leache

Collaborators
  Mitarbeiter
Federico Rodríguez Parets,
Miguel Muñoz, Xabier Aguirre,
Iñigo Beguiristáin

Technical architects
  Ausführungsplanung
José Luis Sola, Arturo Pérez

Structural engineer
  Tragwerk
Ove Arup & Partners, Madrid

Mechanical engineer
  Haustechnik
Ove Arup & Partners, Madrid

Cross section
Querschnitt

Longitudinal section
Längsschnitt

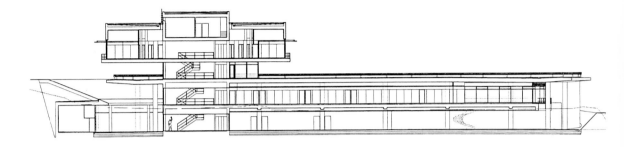

Site plan
Lageplan

Plan, level 1: offices
Grundriß Ebene 1: Büros

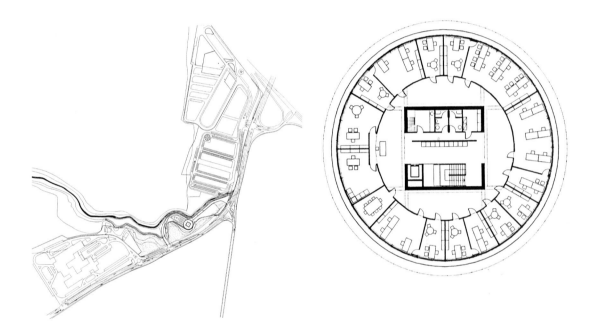

Plan, level -1: locker rooms,
briefing, labs
Grundriß Ebene -1: Spindräume,
Einsatzzentrale, Labors

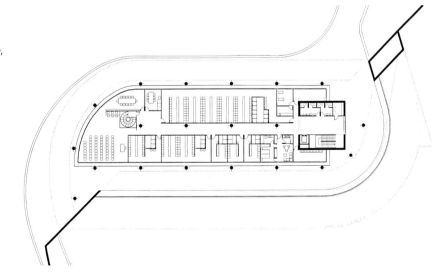

Jesús Irisarri & Guadalupe Piñera Vigo

The northwestern region of Galicia is a difficult place for young architects to get a start. There are few open competitions for public buildings or housing, and the indifference of the private sector to architectural quality, general in most of the country, is augmented here by poverty and by aggressive speculative development that has met few regulatory controls. Galicia's isolation and poverty are compensated by plentiful local materials and crafts, including stone, wood and ship-building metal arts, and by a landscape with a powerful identity of place, arising from a varied topography and a long history of settlement. Despite the inevitable impact of these regional factors, Jesús Irisarri and Guadalupe Piñera look beyond issues of regionalism or local identity in their designs. They develop each project from a general idea, such as the theme of lightness in the Segade House, the fracturing of the facades of the S. Jurjo Badia Street Apartments, or the assimilation of various Modernist legacies in an early work such as the Villamarín Medical Clinic. They maintain an ongoing interest in experimental building materials, often industrial grade or from the world of budget-speculative construction. And they have explored other techniques to make the most of clients' limited funds, such as the incorporation of passive climatization concepts in the recently completed Losada School in Vigo, which have virtually eliminated the need for heating, according to the architects.

In der spanischen Nordwestregion Galicien ist es für einen jungen Architekten schwer, seine Karriere zu beginnen. Es gibt nur wenige offene Wettbewerbe um öffentliche Gebäude und Wohnungsbau und die Gleichgültigkeit des Privatsektors gegenüber architektonischer Qualität, die in weiten Teilen des Landes verbreitet ist, wird hier noch durch die Armut und die aggressive, kaum kontrollierte Immobilienspekulation verstärkt.

Galiciens Isolation und Armut wird von reichen lokalen Materialien und Handwerkstraditionen aufgewogen, darunter Stein-, Holz- und Metallverarbeitung im Schiffbau, sowie durch eine Landschaft mit einer kraftvollen Identität, die sich einer abwechslungsreichen Topographie und langen Siedlungsgeschichte verdankt.

Trotz des unvermeidlichen Einflusses dieser regionalen Faktoren zielen Jesús Irisarri und Guadalupe Piñera in ihren Entwürfen über die Themen des Regionalismus und der lokalen Identität hinaus. Sie entwickeln jedes Projekt aus einer allgemeinen Idee, wie dem Thema der Leichtigkeit beim Segade-Haus, der Fassadenkomposition der Apartments in der S. Jurjo Badia-Straße oder der Assimilation verschiedener Elemente des modernen Architekturerbes in einer frühen Arbeit wie der Medizinischen Klinik Villamarín. Sie bewahren sich dabei ein fortlaufendes Interesse für experimentelle Baustoffe, häufig industrieller Herkunft oder aus der Welt des kostensparenden spekulativen Bauens. Und sie haben andere Techniken erkundet, um das Beste aus den begrenzten Budgets ihrer Klienten zu machen, wie etwa die passive Klimatisierung in der kürzlich fertiggestellten Losada-Schule in Vigo, die den Architekten zufolge eine Heizung praktisch überflüssig macht.

Medical Clinic   Villamarín (Orense), 1989–1991
Klinik

A pair of stone walls define the precinct of this small rural clinic amid its wild natural surroundings: a curving wall skirts the building to the south, protecting the staggered facades of the examination rooms, while the circulation spine to the north is defined by a long straight wall, penetrated by small openings of glass block and topped by a continuous clerestory, with a zone of services enclosed in a parallel wall beyond it. The configuration of a circulation spine that organizes the staggered perpendicular slots of space comprising the waiting areas and examination rooms recalls the plans of Alvaro Aalto, or some of the post-Prairie Style houses of Frank Lloyd Wright, as do the textures of stone and wood, the inclined ceilings and clerestory light. The image of stone walls extending into the landscape, and engulfed and occupied by the building, re-interprets the type forms of Galician farmyards and rural constructions, a theme which Portuguese architect Eduardo Souto Moura has taken up in more Miesian terms in his houses in nearby Porto.

Zwei Steinmauern definieren den Bezirk dieser kleinen Landklinik mitten in der Natur: Eine geschwungene Mauer faßt das Gebäude im Süden ein und schützt die gestaffelten Fassaden der Untersuchungsräume, während die Erschließungsachse im Norden von einer langen, geraden Mauer mit kleinen Öffnungen aus Glasbausteinen definiert wird. Gekrönt von einem durchlaufenden Obergaden, bildet sie mit einer parallelen Wand dahinter die Seitenwände eines Service-Bereichs.

Die Figur der Erschließungsachse, die die versetzten, rechtwinklig dazu verlaufenden Räume organisiert, in denen die Wartebereiche und die Untersuchungsräume untergebracht sind, erinnert an Grundrisse von Alvaro Aalto oder an einige der nach der Präriestilphase entstandenen Häuser von Frank Lloyd Wright, ebenso wie die Texturen von Stein und Holz, die geneigten Decken und die Belichtung von oben mit natürlichem Licht. Das Bild der Steinmauern, die sich in die Landschaft hineinschieben mit dem Gebäude in der Mitte, interpretiert die typologischen Formen galicischer Höfe und Landwirtschaftsgebäude auf neue Weise, ein Thema, das der portugiesische Architekt Eduardo Souto Moura in einem stärker an Mies van der Rohe erinnernden Stil bei seinen Häusern in der Nähe von Porto aufgenommen hat.

South elevation
Südfassade

General view from south
Gesamtansicht von Süden

Client
  Auftraggeber
SERGAS, Xunta of Galicia

Technical architect
  Kostenkontrolle
Ignacio Urrutia

Builder
  Generalunternehmer
Ferreiro

Photos
  Fotos
Leopoldo Alonso-Lamberti

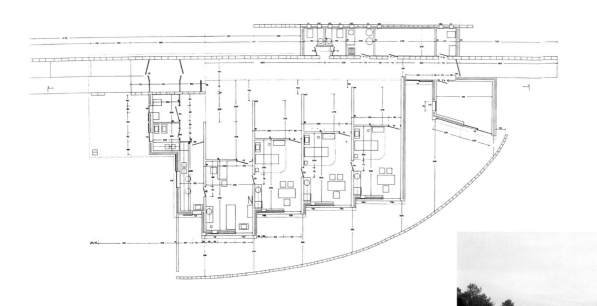

Floor plan

Grundriß

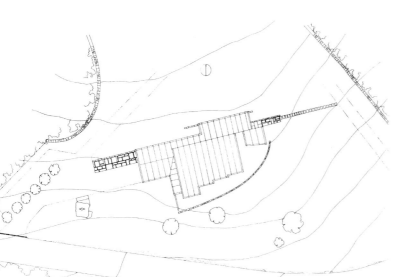

Site plan

Grundstücksplan

North elevation

Nordfassade

Entry porch

Eingangsportal

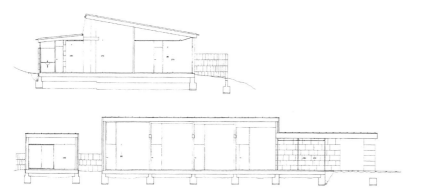

Nort-south section through waiting area (left) and consulting room (right)

East-west section through entry (right) and waiting area

Nord-Süd-Schnitt durch den Wartebereich (links) und Sprech-zimmer (rechts)

Ost-West-Schnitt durch den Eingangs- (rechts) und Warte-bereich

S. Jurjo Badia Street Apartments   Vigo, 1991–1994
Apartments S. Jurjo Badia-Straße

Street facade
Straßenfassade

Interior window wall
Innere Fensterwand

Stair, top floor duplex
Treppe, Duplexwohnung
Obergeschoß

This privately-promoted building contains five floors of residential apartments over a ground floor bakery and mezzanine offices. The design attempts to bring a measure of dignity to an urban context degraded by low-quality speculative development. The deep and narrow configuration of the site arises from its origins in an urban texture of low-rise houses and gardens facing narrow streets, subsequently redeveloped to higher densities. The ground floor is set two meters back from the building line to create a wider sidewalk area. The cantilever of the upper body of the building is supported by a freestanding round column that continues through the remaining floors. Upper facades are angled so as to be oriented towards longer views parallel to the street. The small apartments are relatively diaphanous and ambiguous in layout in order to maximize the penetration of natural light and the flexibility of uses. Duplex units occupy the top two floors.

Dieses privatfinanzierte Gebäude umfaßt fünf Geschosse mit Wohnungen über einer Bäckerei im Erdgeschoß und Halbgeschoß-büros. Der Entwurf versucht, dem urbanen Kontext, der durch spekulative Bauten von geringer Qualität verschandelt ist, ein Maß an Würde zurückzugeben. Die tiefe und enge Grundrißform ergibt sich aus der vorherr-schenden später verdichteten Bebauung mit niedrigen Häusern und engen Gärten zur Straße hin.

Das Erdgeschoß ist zwei Meter von der Fassadenflucht zurückgesetzt, um einen breite-ren Bürgersteig zu schaffen. Die Auskragung

Client
 Auftraggeber
Delmiro Vidal

Collaborators
 Mitarbeiter
Javier Rivas Barros,
Antonio González

Technical architect
 Ausführungsplanung
José Areal Benavides

Structural engineer
 Tragwerk
Ramón Lago

Builder
 Generalunternehmer
Delmiro Vidal

Photos
 Fotos
Leopoldo Alonso-Lamberti,
Manuel G. Vicente

Levels 2 & 3 plan
Grundriß Niveaus 2 und 3

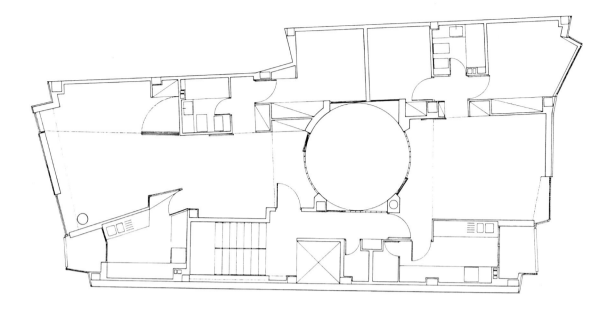

Ground level plan
Grundriß Erdgeschoß

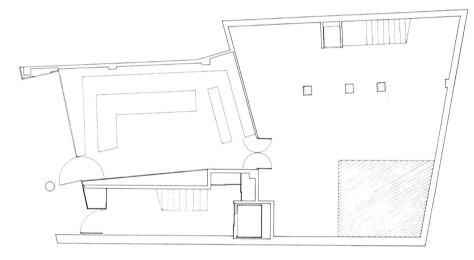

Section
Querschnitt

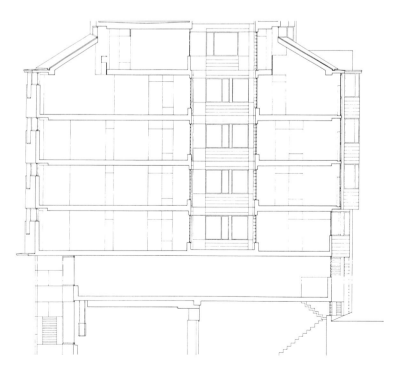

des oberen Gebäudeteils wird von einer freistehenden runden
Säule gestützt, die sich über die übrigen Stockwerke fortsetzt.
Die oberen Fassaden sind abgewinkelt, um weitere Ausblicke
die Straße entlang zu bieten. Die schmalen Apartments sind
relativ lichtdurchlässig und in ihrer Gestaltung variabel, um
einen maximalen Einfall an natürlichem Licht und eine flexible Nutzung zu ermöglichen. Die beiden Obergeschosse bestehen aus Maisonnettewohnungen.

Segade House   Fragosela (Vigo), 1996
Haus Segade

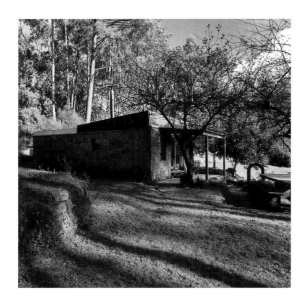

Exterior
Außenansicht

Bedroom
corridor
Schlafzimmer-
korridor

The renovation and enlargement of this small stone house, located on a wooded hillside five minutes by car from Vigo and used as a year-round residence, was financed by a grant from the regional government dedicated to the conservation and improvement of traditional rural houses. A wing containing kitchen, bath and three small bedrooms was added to the back of the original stone enclosure, enlarging the dwelling from 50 to 90 m². The architects experimented with exterior finishes normally employed in industrial buildings in order to minimize costs, to create a light-weight contrast to the stone, and to permit large openings of glass, notably lacking in traditional constructions. Boards composed of a mixture of cement and wood fiber are used as the exterior skin for the ventilated cavity walls of the new wing. The structural wall behind this skin is brick, finished in stucco on the interiors. The new roof over the stone enclosure incorporates a south-facing clerestory, and is covered in two layers of asphaltic felt to suggest a tensile, inflated structure. The bedroom wing roof is finished in a folded aluminum sheet.

Die Renovierung und Erweiterung dieses kleinen Steinhauses an einem waldigen Hügel fünf Autominuten von Vigo entfernt, das ganzjährig als Wohnhaus genutzt wird, wurde mit Mitteln der Regionalregierung finanziert, mit denen traditionelle Landhäuser bewahrt und in ihrer Substanz verbessert werden sollen. Ein Flügel mit Küche, Bad und drei kleinen Schlafzimmern wurde dem ursprünglichen Steinhaus hinzugefügt, so daß sich die Wohnfläche von 50 auf 90 m² vergrößerte.

Um einen leichtgewichtigen Kontrast zum Steingebäude zu schaffen und große Glasöffnungen zu ermöglichen, die in der lokalen Architektur auffallend abwesend sind, experimentierten die Architekten mit einer Behandlung der Außenfassaden, die gewöhnlich bei Industriegebäuden verwendet wird, um die Kosten zu minimieren. Paneele, die aus einer Mischung von Beton und Holzfasern bestehen, werden als Außenhaut der belüfteten Hohlwände des neuen Flügels eingesetzt. Die tragende Wand dahinter besteht aus Ziegeln, die innen verputzt sind. Das neue Dach über der Steinummauerung schließt einen nach Süden ausgerichteten Lichtgaden ein und ist mit zwei Lagen Dachpappe abgedeckt. Das Dach des Schlafzimmerflügels ist mit gewelltem Aluminium abgedeckt.

Clients
Auftraggeber
Sara Segade & Jorge Berridy

Builder
Generalunternehmer
Norte

Photos
Fotos
Manuel G. Vicente

Joint between stone wall and
bedroom wing

Steinmauer und Schlafzimmerflügel

Living area towards kitchen

Wohnzimmer mit Blick zur Küche

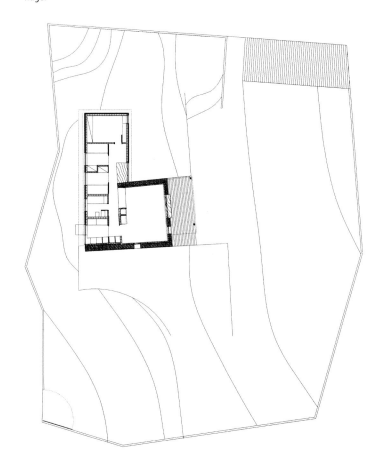

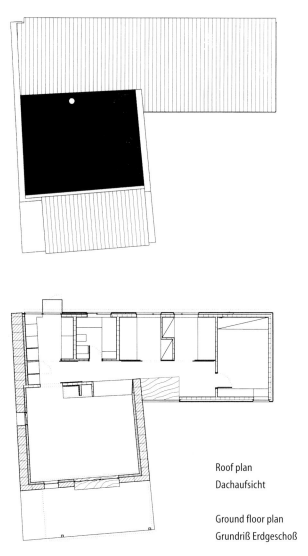

Roof plan

Dachaufsicht

Site plan

Grundstücksplan

Ground floor plan

Grundriß Erdgeschoß

Living area

Wohnbereich

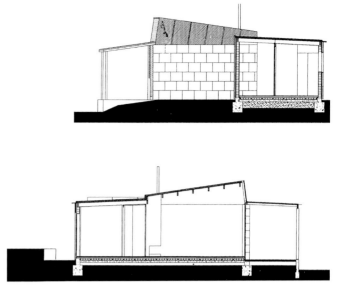

Top: South-north section through bedroom wing
Bottom: North-south section through kitchen (left), living area and porch (right)

Oben: Süd-Nord-Schnitt durch Schlafzimmerflügel
Unten: Nord-Süd-Schnitt. Links: Küche; rechts: Wohnbereich, Veranda

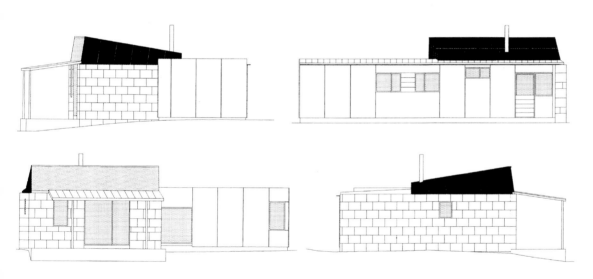

Top: East elevation, north elevation

Bottom: South elevation, west elevation

Oben: Aufriß Ostseite, Aufriß Nordseite

Unten: Aufriß Südseite, Aufriß Westseite

Pura García Márquez, Luis Rubiño, Ignacio Rubiño Sevilla

While still students in the mid-eighties, García, Rubiño and Rubiño (GRR) served their apprenticeship in the studios of Seville's leading architects, Cruz & Ortiz and Guillermo Vázquez Consuegra. They opened their own office on graduating in 1986. Despite the spectacular public works carried out for the 1992 Expo, Seville remains the center of one of Spain's poorer regions. For Francisco Mangado, observing their work from the relatively prosperous north of Pamplona,[1] the scarcity of opportunities in the region has led GRR to practice "an architecture of survival," in which the harshness of the climate, minimal budgets and cultural apathy leave only a "narrow margin for manoeuver" in the struggle to "induce an architecture of a certain quality."

Ignacio Rubiño does not see his studio's position as quite so beleaguered, however. He explains that Andalucía is characterized by a "degraded present with a rich past," and that its inhabitants, "in a physical landscape populated with deficiencies, have always sought poetry in other dimensions." This indirect poetry and rich legacy are present in even the most modest of the firm's work, their public housing projects. Rubiño explains that GRR do not seek to impose an architectural aesthetic on the unknown clients of subsidized housing. Rather, they aim for a certain neutrality, and cede to the residents' right to stylistically modify the works over time, as inevitably happens. But though true to legal restrictions, limited means and public indifference, this apparently transparent methodology produces an architecture that is unmistakably of its place and time. Identity and culture, their work seems to suggest, are something that one doesn't have to struggle for; like the poetry of another dimension, they are simply, ineffably in the air.

Noch während ihres Studiums Mitte der 80er Jahre arbeiteten García, Rubiño und Rubiño (GRR) für Sevillas führende Architekten Cruz & Ortiz und Guillermo Vázquez Consuegra. Nach ihrem Diplom 1986 eröffneten sie ihr eigenes Büro. Trotz der spektakulären öffentlichen Bauten, die 1992 für die Expo geschaffen wurden, bleibt Sevilla das Zentrum einer der ärmsten Regionen Spaniens. Für Francisco Mangado, der ihre Arbeit aus dem relativ wohlhabenden nördlichen Pamplona verfolgt,[1] haben die geringen Möglichkeiten der Region GRR dazu gebracht, eine „Architektur des Überlebens" zu praktizieren, bei der die Härte des Klimas, die geringen Budgets und die kulturelle Apathie für den Kampf um „eine Architektur von einer gewissen Qualität" nur einen „engen Spielraum" lasse.

Ignacio Rubiño sieht jedoch die Lage seines Büros nicht ganz so dramatisch. Andalusien, so erklärt er, charakterisiere eine „heruntergekommene Gegenwart und eine reiche Vergangenheit"; es sei eine Region, deren Einwohner „angesichts der Defizite ihrer physischen Umgebung Poesie immer in anderen Dimensionen gesucht haben". Eine entsprechend indirekte Poesie und das reiche Erbe der Region sind selbst noch in den bescheidensten Werken der Architekten, ihren öffentlichen Wohnbauten, präsent. Rubiño zufolge versucht GRR nicht, den unbekannten Bewohnern öffentlicher Wohnbauten eine Architekturästhetik aufzuzwingen. Statt dessen zielen sie auf eine gewisse Neutralität und räumen den Bewohnern das Recht ein, ihre Gebäude mit der Zeit stilistisch zu verändern, was unweigerlich geschieht. Aber obwohl diese scheinbar klare Methodologie mit rechtlichen Beschränkungen, begrenzten Mitteln und einer gleichgültigen Öffentlichkeit zu rechnen hat, gehört sie unverwechselbar ihrem Ort und ihrer Zeit an. Identität und Kultur, so scheinen die Arbeiten von GRR nahezulegen, sind etwas, für das man nicht kämpfen muß; wie die Poesie einer anderen Dimension liegen sie einfach und unaussprechlich in der Luft.

1 Works 1989/1997: Ignacio Rubiño Luis Rubiño Pura García, "Architectures de Autor," 1998

Public Housing   Los Palacios (Seville), 1989–1996
Soziale Wohnbauten

General view
Blick in die Siedlung

At the edge of an agricultural town 24 km south of Seville, and bordering marshlands destined for a future park, 136 units of low-cost public housing are arranged along a linear sequence of irregular pedestrian streets and spaces.

The innovative unit type draws on traditional formal strategies that respond to local living patterns and the severe climate. Two, three and four-bedroom units are developed from the same ground floor plan, in which a narrow passage from the pedestrian street leads to a central patio with entries to the living area and hall. A second access leads through a rear patio to the kitchen. The ground floor "bedroom" can be used for an elder parent or informal living area. The third and fourth bedrooms on the upper floor are added incrementally, filling a high-walled roof terrace.

The central patio adds livable space to the units without exceeding public housing norms. Many occupants have covered it with canvas or canes, as in traditional homes. The incremental growth of the plan type allows owners of smaller units to add space over time. The architects consider their design as a base, both spatially and stylistically, to be adapted by the owners to their different needs and tastes.

Am Rande einer landwirtschaftlich geprägten Stadt 24 Kilometer südlich von Sevilla arrangierten die Architekten 136 Wohneinheiten als kostengünstige soziale Wohnbauten entlang einer linearen Sequenz ungleichmäßiger Fußgängerstraßen und Außenräume.

Die innovative Mustereinheit schöpft aus traditionellen formalen Strategien, die auf lokalen Lebensgewohnheiten und dem strengen Klima beruhen. Einheiten mit zwei, drei und vier Schlafzimmern werden aus dem gleichen Erdgeschoßgrundriß entwickelt, bei dem ein schmaler Durchgang von einer Fußgängerstraße zu einem zentralen Patio mit den Eingängen zum Flur und dem Wohnzimmer führt. Ein zweiter Zugang führt durch einen rückwärtigen Patio in die Küche. Im „Schlafzimmer" im Erdgeschoß kann beispielsweise ein hilfsbedürftiges Elternteil untergebracht werden, oder es kann als informelles Wohnzimmer genutzt werden. Ein drittes und viertes Zimmer lassen sich später im Obergeschoß anstelle der Dachterrasse mit seiner hohen Brüstung hinzufügen.

Durch den zentralen Patio gewinnen die Einheiten zusätzlichen Raum, ohne die Normen für den öffentlichen Wohnungsbau zu überschreiten. Viele Bewohner haben ihn wie bei tradi-

Client
  Auftraggeber
Department of Public Works and Transport, Junta of Andalucia

Collaborators
  Mitarbeit
Oscar Gil Delgado, 1st phase

Technical architects
  Ausführungsplanung
Robert Alés; with Juan Merchante, 1st phase

Structural engineer
  Tragwerk
O. Gil Delgado

Mechanical engineer
  Haustechnik
F. García Martín

Builder
  Generalunternehmer
Antonio del Ojo, 1st phase; Fomento de Construcciones y Contratas (FCC)

Photos
  Fotos
Duccio Malagamba

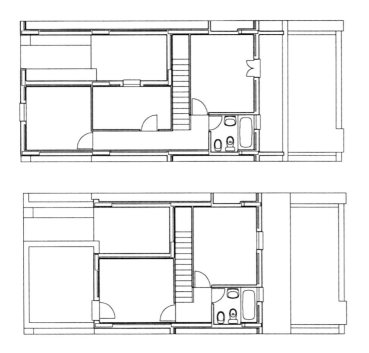

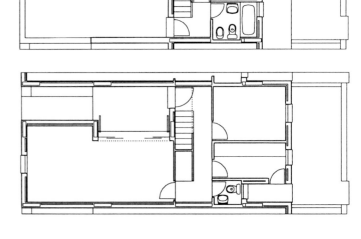

Unit plans: Top floor, 4 bedrooms; top floor, 3 bedrooms

Grundrisse der Wohneinheiten: Obergeschoß der Einheit mit vier und drei Schlafzimmern

Top floor, 2 bedrooms; ground floor

Obergeschoß der Einheit mit zwei Schlafzimmern; Erdgeschoß

Typical block plan and section
Regelgrundriß des Blocks und Schnitt

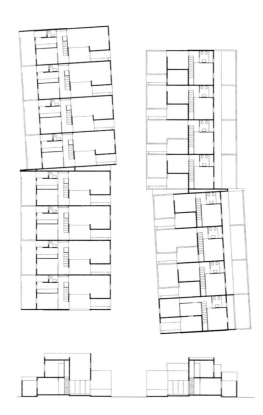

Typical pedestrian street
Typische Fußgängerstraße

tionellen Häusern mit Zeltbahnen oder Rohr abgedeckt. Das additive Wachstum des Mustergrundrisses erlaubt den Besitzern kleinerer Einheiten, sich mit der Zeit zu vergrößern. Die Architekten betrachten ihre Gestaltung als Basis, die es den Besitzern gestattet, sie sowohl räumlich wie stilistisch ihren Bedürfnissen und ihrem Geschmack anzupassen

Bonsor Museum and House, Luna Castle   Mairena de Alcor (Seville), 1994–
Bonsor Museum und Haus, Burg Luna

Model, interior of archives

Modellansicht des Archivinnen-
raums

The English traveler George Bonsor, pioneer of modern archeology in Andalucia, restored the 13th century Luna Castle for his home and collections at the turn of the century. This project for the regional government consolidates his legacy. Bonsor built his residence between two of the four corner towers in the castle precinct. The architects have introduced a semi-buried exhibit room in an existing trench between the two towers facing the residence, and a raised archives pavilion to one side.

The exhibit space is naturally lit from clerestories, and follows the irregular outline of the castle wall to define different permanent display areas. An underground grain silo found during the excavations is penetrated by a descending stair.

Construction elements are preassembled and raised to the site so as not to disturb a protected colony of birds living

Der englische Reisende George Bonsor, Pionier der modernen Archäologie in Andalusien, restaurierte um die Jahrhundertwende die Burg Luna aus dem 13. Jahrhundert, um darin zu wohnen und seine Sammlungen unterzubringen. Dieser Entwurf im Auftrag der Regionalregierung bewahrt sein Vermächtnis. Bonsor baute seine Residenz zwischen zwei der vier Ecktürme des Burgareals. In einem vorhandenen Graben zwischen den beiden Türmen gegenüber diesem Wohnbau haben die Architekten einen halb in die Erde versenkten Ausstellungsraum und einen erhöhten Archivpavillon hinzugefügt.

Der Ausstellungsraum wird durch Oberlichter natürlich erhellt und folgt dem unregelmäßigen Verlauf der Burgmauer, um verschiedene Bereiche der Dauerausstellung zu definieren. Ein unterirdisches Getreidesilo, das während der Ausgrabungen entdeckt wurde, wird von einer nach unten führenden Treppe durchstoßen.

Client
  Auftraggeber
Department of Culture,
Junta of Andalucía

Technical architect
  Ausführungsplanung
Robert Alés

Structural engineer
  Tragwerk
O. Gil Delgado

Photos
  Fotos
Fernando Alda

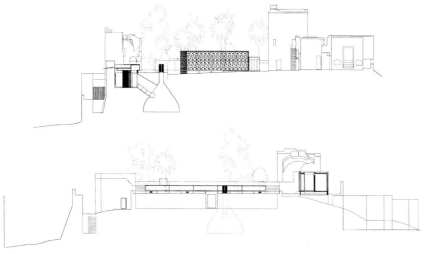

General sections/elevations: Top, left to right: Section, exhibit hall; elevation, archives; Bottom, left to right: Elevation, exhibit hall; section, archives

Schnitte und Aufrisse: Oben, von links nach rechts: Schnitt durch Ausstellungshalle; Aufriß Archivpavillon; Unten, von links nach rechts: Aufriß Ausstellungshalle; Schnitt durch Archiv

General plan

Gesamtplan

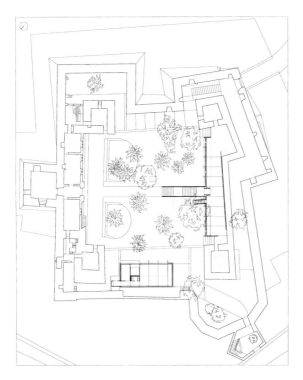

Model, interior of exhibit hall

Model, semi-buried exhibition hall

Castle and town, circa 1902. Present state of castle is similar

Modell des Innenraums der Ausstellungshalle

Modellansicht der halbversenkten Ausstellungshalle

Burg und Stadt, zirka 1902. Der heutige Zustand der Burg ist ähnlich.

in the ruins. Materials and colors are chosen to harmonize with the fragile sandstone of the geologic outcropping and the battlements rising out of it. The main facade of the archive is a perforated ceramic screen composed of two-meter long glazed and fired red clay panels. Precast concrete planks have been used to form vertical screens and horizontal ceiling baffles.

Die Bauelemente wurden vormontiert zum Bauplatz gebracht und von oben eingesetzt, um eine in den Ruinen lebende Vogelkolonie nicht zu stören. Materialien und Farben wurden so gewählt, daß sie mit dem weichen Sandstein des Untergrundes und den Zinnen harmonieren, die sich über ihm erheben. Die Hauptfassade des Archivpavillons ist eine perforierte Keramikverblendung aus zwei Meter langen glasierten und gebrannten Tonscheiben. Vorgefertigte Betonplanken wurden für die Wände und Decken verwendet.

Jaén Football Stadium   Jaén, 1998–
Jaén Fußballstadion

Model	Study model, tribune grandstand
Modell	Studienmodell der überdachten Tribüne

Despite its enormous scale and impact, the design intent was to integrate the stadium into the surrounding landscape of hills covered with olive trees. The stadium's outlines respect the curving typography, while the playing field and grandstands are sunken below the level of the terrain, using to advantage excavated gravel pits on the site.

Following the custom of local agricultural installations, the architects first established a defined exterior precinct, and then arranged the various elements of the tribune, entries, lighting towers, gardens etc. as smaller elements within it. Many walls and structures are faced in brick, a characteristic local finish.

Trotz seiner enormen Ausmaße und Wirkung war es die Gestaltungsabsicht, das Stadion in die umliegende, von Olivenbäumen bedeckte Hügellandschaft zu integrieren. Die Konturen des Stadions respektieren die gewellte Topographie, während das Spielfeld und die überdachten Tribünen unter das Bodenniveau des Terrains abgesenkt wurden, wobei schon vorhandene Kiesgruben auf dem Grundstück genutzt werden konnten.

Der lokalen ländlichen Bautradition folgend definierten die Architekten zunächst eine äußere Begrenzung und arrangierten dann die verschiedenen Elemente der Tribüne, Eingänge, Lichttürme, Gärten etc. als kleinere Elemente in ihrem Inneren. Viele Wände und tragende Teile sind mit Ziegel verkleidet, ein charakteristisches lokales Fassadenmaterial.

Client
Auftraggeber
Public Land Development Company of Andalucía

Technical architects
Kostenkontrolle
Análisis de Edificación y Construcción

Builder
Generalunternehmer
Agroman

Photos
Fotos
Fernando Alda

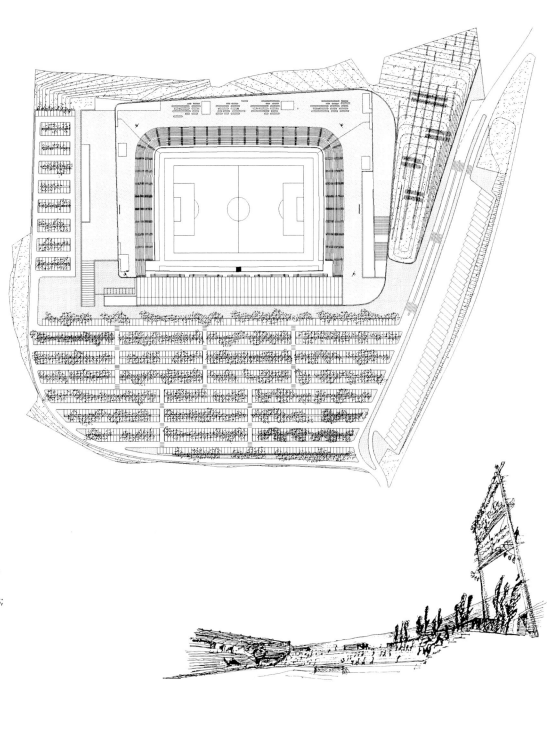

Top: View from playing field;
tribune at right

Oben: Blick vom Spielfeld aus;
rechts Tribüne

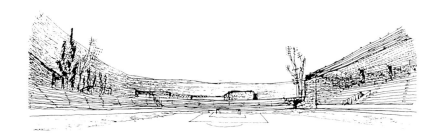

Overlooking stadium towards
Jaén from promenade deck

Entry to grandstands

Blick vom Promenadendeck über
das Stadium Richtung Jaén

Eingang zu den Tribünen

General section through stands
and playing field

Schnitt durch Tribünen und
Spielfeld

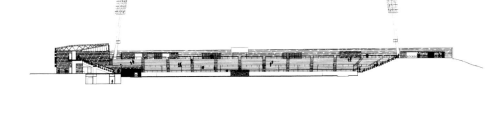

Side elevation

Seitenansicht

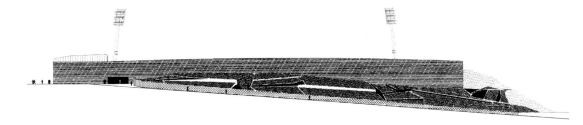

Javier García-Solera, Alfredo Payá Alicante

The two architects form a loose alliance, working sometimes together, sometimes independently, and sometimes with others. García-Solera is also a frequent collaborator with Lola Alonso (Alicante, 1951) on projects such as the Bernabué Medical Institute and the Alicante Institute for Small and Medium Businesses. The three have even competed against one another: in the recent competition for the Alicante School of Architecture, Payá won an honorable mention, García-Solera's project was a finalist, and Alonso won the job.

The positive creative energy produced by this mixture of comradeship and friendly rivalry is reflected in their work. In the Museum for the University of Alicante, Payá uses pared-down abstract forms as elements in a dramatic, poetic unfolding of the architectural promenade, an experiential poetics with affinities to Spanish architect Alberto Campo Baeza. At the adjacent Business School, García-Solera develops a more cool and formalist abstraction from the clear expression of structure and function. Of this work he has said, "the smooth planar surfaces, pure forms, basic geometry and neutral colors are testimony to the value of abstraction as a universal language."

Their work in partnership brings these complementary sensibilities together, in designs whose expressive power resides in their enigmatic restraint and rigor. Many projects explore the theme of the inwardly-focused building or compound, which seeks refuge from a hot summer climate and harsh surroundings in an interiority modulated by indirect infusions of natural light.

Die beiden Architekten bilden eine lose Allianz, arbeiten manchmal zusammen, manchmal allein und zuweilen mit anderen Architekten. García-Solera arbeitet außerdem häufig mit Lola Alonso (Alicante, 1951) an Projekten wie dem Medizinischen Institut Bernabué und dem Institut für Mittelständische Unternehmen von Alicante. Die drei konkurrieren sogar miteinander: Beim jüngsten Wettbewerb für die Architekturschule von Alicante wurde Payás Entwurf lobend erwähnt, Garcia-Soleras kam in die engere Auswahl und Alonso erhielt den Zuschlag.

Die positive kreative Energie, die aus dieser Mischung aus Freundschaft und freundlicher Rivalität entsteht, spiegelt sich in ihren Arbeiten. Beim Museum für die Universität von Alicante benutzt Payá reduzierte abstrakte Formen als Elemente einer dramatischen, poetischen Präsentation einer Architekturpromenade, eine experimentelle Poetik mit einer Affinität zum spanischen Architekten Alberto Campo Baeza. In der angrenzenden Business School entwickelt García aus dem klaren konstruktiven und funktionalen Ausdruck eine kühlere und formalistischere Abstraktion. „Die ebenen Flächen, die reinen Formen, die grundlegende Geometrie und die neutralen Farben bezeugen", so sagt García über diese Arbeit, „den Wert der Abstraktion als universelle Sprache".

Ihre Partnerschaft bringt diese komplementären Sensibilitäten in Entwürfen zusammen, deren expressive Kraft in ihrer enigmatischen Zurückhaltung und Strenge liegt. Viele Projekte erkunden das Thema des nach innen gewandten Gebäudes oder Ensembles, das vor einem heißen Sommerklima und unwirtlichen Umgebungen in einer durch indirektes natürliches Licht modulierten Innerlichkeit Zuflucht sucht.

Office Building, Diputación Provincial   Alicante, 1985–1996
Bürogebäude der Diputación Provincial

Aerial view
Luftbild

Facade
Fassade

The building is an office annex to the seat of provincial government, located in the Castista Palace across the street. The architects offer a radical solution to the challenge of bringing natural light and ventilation into the narrow urban plot, which has a western exposure 20 meters wide and is 42 meters deep. The building is cut from top to bottom and end to end by two narrow light trenches with an east-west orientation, one running through the center of the plot and the other at its northern border. The slots allow interior spaces to "search to the north for reflected southern light," in the words of the architects, and divide each of the five floors into four symmetrical open-plan office zones. Vertical circulation occupies a transverse zone bridging the light slots at the center of the building, and horizontal circulation runs on either side of the central trough. The western facade is a

Das Gebäude ist ein ergänzender Bürobau für den Sitz der Provinzregierung im Schloß Castista auf der anderen Straßenseite. Die Architekten fanden eine radikale Lösung für die Herausforderung, auf dem schmalen städtischen Grundstück, das an seiner Westseite 20 Meter breit und 42 Meter tief ist, für natürliches Licht und Belüftung zu sorgen. Das Gebäude wird in Ost-West-Richtung von oben bis unten und von einer zur anderen Seite von zwei engen Lichtschlitzen durchschnitten; einer verläuft durch das Zentrum des Grundstücks, der andere an seiner nördlichen Grenze. Durch die Schlitze können die Innenräume „im Norden nach reflektiertem Südlicht suchen", wie es die Architekten ausdrücken. Sie teilen jedes der fünf Geschosse in vier symmetrische Bürozonen mit offenem Grundriß. Die vertikale Erschließung verläuft quer zu den Lichtschlitzen, während die horizontale Erschließung zu beiden

Client
  Auftraggeber
Provincial Government of
  Alicante

Architects
  Architekten
Javier García-Solera, Alfredo Payá

Structural engineer
  Tragwerk
Domingo Sepulcre

Technical architects
  Ausführungsplanung
Fernando Cortés, Marcos Gallud

Builder
  Generalunternehmer
ECISA

Photos
  Fotos
Hisao Suzuki

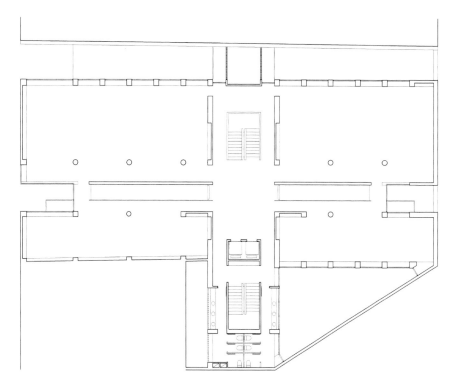

Typical floor plan
Regelgrundriß

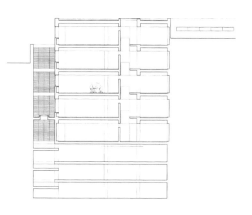

Transverse north-south section
Querschnitt in Nord-Süd-Richtung

Typical office suite
Musterbüro

simple reflection of this organization, with the entry recessed into the central crevice.

The scheme is an interesting variation on the traditional but overly-dense organization of many Spanish urban buildings around a series of patios. It captures the intermingling of interior and exterior space characteristic of such buildings, shredding conventional notions of vertical and horizontal spatial containment.

Seiten des zentralen Einschnitts untergebracht ist. Die Westfassade ist eine schlichte Spiegelung dieser Organisation, wobei der Eingang zurückversetzt in der zentralen Spalte liegt.

Dieses Schema ist eine interessante Variation der traditionellen, aber allzu dichten Organisation vieler spanischer Stadtgebäude um eine Reihe von Patios. Es fängt die für solche Gebäude charakteristische Vermischung von Innen- und Außenraum ein und kümmert sich nicht um konventionelle Begriffe von vertikaler und horizontaler räumlicher Begrenzung.

Alicante University Museum   Alicante, 1994–1997
Museum der Universität Alicante

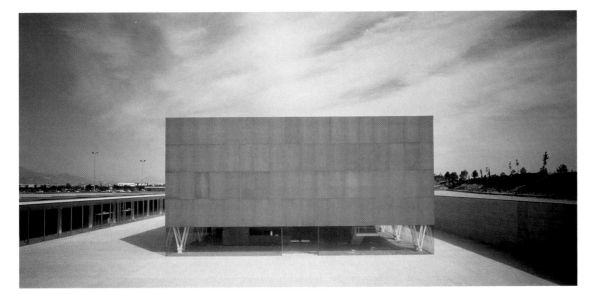

Exhibit pavilion in sunken patio

Ausstellungspavillon im abgesenkten Patio

The building is arranged around a sunken patio, in retreat from its noisy site beside a highway at the edge of the university campus. From the street, only the closed upper volume of the central exhibit pavilion is visible, rising from the excavation and mirrored in the reflective surface of the flooded ground plane, apparently inaccessible.

The complex is reached via a partially covered descending ramp. From the travertine-walled patio, in turn, the visitor's gaze is projected over the bleak surroundings to distant, arid mountains and the sky.

Polyvalent exhibit rooms line one side of the patio behind a continuous plane of glass, their skylights poking above the flooded roof. The adjacent auditorium is mirrored in an outdoor amphitheater. The glass wall between them can be folded away to join the spaces.

The central exhibit pavilion is composed of a wood volume suspended, apparently weightless, over the void of a frameless horizontal glass wall. Its exterior is finished in nautical plywood with a tropical veneer. The thick cavity wall enclosing the supporting trusses is accessible for mechanical services and mounting displays and audio-visual projections.

Das Gebäude gliedert sich um einen abgesenkten Patio, der sich von der lauten, vielbefahrenen Autobahn am Rande des Universitätsgeländes abkehrt. Von der Straße aus ist nur das geschlossene obere Volumen des zentralen Ausstellungspavillons sichtbar, das sich aus der Absenkung erhebt und – scheinbar unzugänglich – in der ebenerdigen Wasserfläche spiegelt. Der Komplex ist über eine absteigende, zum Teil überdachte Rampe zugänglich. Im Patio mit seinen Travertinwänden kann der Besucher den Blick in den Himmel und in die karge Umgebung bis zu den entfernten, trockenen Bergen schweifen lassen.

Vielgestaltige Ausstellungsräume liegen an einer Seite des Patios hinter einer durchlaufenden Glasfassade; ihre Dachfenster erheben sich über das geflutete Dach. Das angrenzende Auditorium spiegelt sich in einem Amphitheater unter freiem Himmel. Die Glaswand zwischen ihnen läßt sich zusammenschieben, um die beiden Räume zu verbinden.

Der zentrale Ausstellungspavillon besteht aus einem Holzvolumen, das scheinbar schwerelos auf einer rahmenlosen horizontalen Glaswand schwebt. Seine Außenfasssade besteht aus Preßholzplatten mit Tropenholzfunier. Die dicke Hohlwand, auf der die Tragbalken ruhen, ist für die Wartung der techni-

Client
  Auftraggeber
University of Alicante

Architect
  Architekt
Alfredo Payá

Student Collaborators
  Studentische Mitarbeiter
Javier García Romero, Marta Orts,
  Paula Queralt, Carle Sentieri

Electrical engineer
  Elektrotechnik
Antonio Sánchez

Air conditioning
  Lüftungstechnik
José Mir

Structural engineer
  Tragwerk
Pascual Sirvent

Builder
  Generalunternehmer
AUCINI

Photos
  Fotos
Jordi Bernardó, Miguel Ángel
  Valero, Alfredo Payá,
  Técnicas Fotográficas

Exhibit pavilion interior

Innenraum des Ausstellungspavillons

Sunken patio from entry ramp

Abgesenkter Patio von der
Eingangsrampe aus gesehen

Sections: Top: Through entry
ramp, middle: Longitudinal
through exhibit pavilion,
bottom: Transverse through
exhibit pavilion

Oben: Schnitt durch Eingangsrampe, Mitte: Längsschnitt durch
Ausstellungspavillon; unten:
Querschnitt durch Ausstellungspavillon

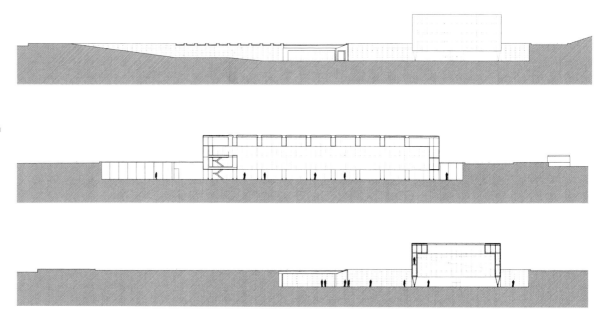

The permanent exhibits are arranged on the ground floor in vitrines and panels. The patio projects a luminous zone of abstract spatial depth into the chamber, in contrast to the more diffuse, floating upper zone defined by the white walls and rooflights.

schen Installationen zugänglich und kann auch für Ausstellungen und audiovisuelle Vorführungen genutzt werden. Die Dauerexponate sind im Erdgeschoß in Vitrinen und Fächern ausgestellt. Der Patio projiziert eine leuchtende Zone abstrakter räumlicher Tiefe ins Innere, im Kontrast zum diffuseren, fließenden oberen Bereich, der von den weißen Wänden und Dachfenstern definiert wird.

Aerial view
Luftbild

Plan
Grundriß

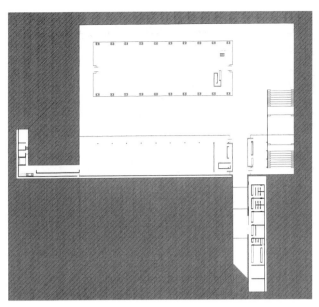

Site plan
Lageplan

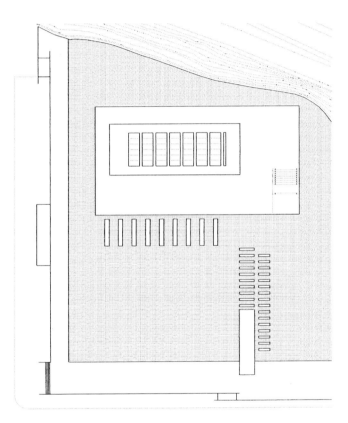

Section through exhibit
pavilion (sketch)

Schnitt durch Ausstellungs–
pavillon (Ideenskizze)

Business School, University of Alicante   Alicante, 1994–1996
Wirtschaftsfakultät, Universität von Alicante

Entry platform, dusk
Interior hall

Eingangsplattform in der
Dämmerung
Innenhalle

Client
  Auftraggeber
University of Alicante

Architect
  Architekt
Javier García-Solera

Technical architects
  Ausführungsplanung
Fernando Cortés, Marcos Gallud

Structural engineer
  Tragwerk
Domingo Sepulcre

Metal structures
  Metallkonstruktion
Juan García-Solera

Builder
  Generalunternehmer
Dragados

Photos
  Fotos
Miguel Ángel Valero
  & Jesús Solera

The Business School is located across the street from Payá's University Museum, and responds to the nearby highway with a similar strategy of interior focus. The U-shaped two-story volume opens through glass walls to its central courtyard, while presenting a hard back of precast concrete panels to the other three sides of the site. A third floor of classrooms is sunken below grade. Beyond a raised and covered entry platform, the central court drops to expose this sunken floor, which also receives light from the eastern exterior exposure via a narrow trench.

The windows lining the courtyard are shaded by screens of pivoting wood louvers. Courtside rooms also present transparent walls to the corridors, orienting interior public spaces towards the court through a succession of translucent veils. On the exterior, the precast floor and wall panels form a clearly legible structural frame that is slightly raised off the ground, a formal gesture that both suggests the presence of the buried floor and dissociates the building from its site.

Die Wirtschaftsfakultät befindet sich auf der anderen Straßenseite gegenüber von Payás Universitätsmuseum und ist wie dieses vor der nahen Autobahn geschützt, indem sie nach innen ausgerichtet ist. Das U-förmige, zweigeschossige Volumen öffnet sich durch Glaswände zu seinem zentralen Hof, während es zu den anderen Seiten des Grundstücks einen harten Rücken aus vorgefertigten Betonpaneelen präsentiert. Ein drittes Geschoß mit Seminarräumen ist unter das Niveau des Erdbodens verlegt. Jenseits einer erhöhten und überdachten Eingangsplattform fällt der zentrale Hof ab und offenbart dieses versenkte Geschoß, das durch einen schmalen Graben auch von der Ostseite Licht erhält.

Die Fenster, die den Hof säumen, werden von verstellbaren Holzblenden beschattet. Die Räume um den Hof zeigen auch zu den Korridoren hin transparente Wände. Öffentliche Räume im Inneren sind so durch eine Abfolge lichtdurchlässiger Schleier auf den Hof ausgerichtet. Außen bilden die vorgefertigten Fußboden- und Wandpaneele ein deutlich lesbares Strukturgerüst, das leicht über den Erdboden angehoben ist, eine formale Geste, die einerseits auf die Gegenwart des unterirdischen Geschosses verweist, andererseits das Gebäude von seinem Grundstück abhebt.

Central court
Zentraler Hof

Ground floor plan
Grundriß Erdgeschoß

Site plan
Lageplan

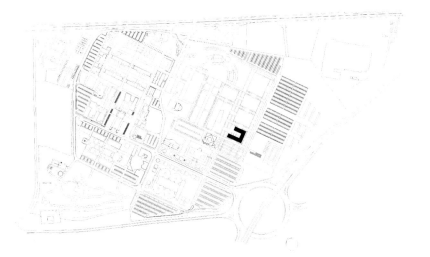

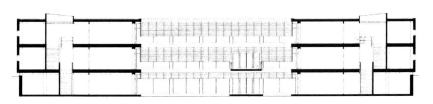

East-west section through patio
South-north section through rear patio

Ost-West-Schnitt durch den Patio
Süd-Nord-Schnitt durch den Patio

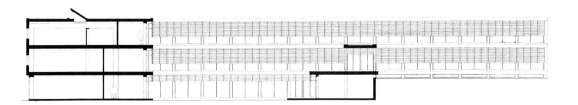

Manuel Feo Las Palmas de Gran Canaria

The distance between the Canary Islands and the rest of Spain is visible in the work of Manuel Feo and his collaborators, which breaks ranks with the generally minimalist tone of their mainland peers. The raw volcanic landscape of the islands, rising violently from the calm horizontal plane of the sea, is transcribed in the angled planes and broken lines of their buildings: the unsquared windows and projecting skylight baffles, the splashes of intense color, the inclined floors, ramps and bowed roofs, the rooflines prolonged by scuppers, drips and peaked, extended eaves, which protect interiors from the vertical African sun.

The Teacher Training College at the University of La Laguna was Feo's first major work with Juan José Espino. Since early 1999 he has formalized his association with Victor Alonso, but he frequently works alone and in collaboration with others as well. Currently, he is building the El Pris Hermitage and other religious projects in Tenerife with Elías Medina. Feo describes his studio as a laboratory that has attracted a loose group of architects and clients interested in experimental design.

Feo cites no direct influences, and his points of reference differ from the mainland's usual sources. The Teacher Training College owes something to Álvaro Siza's spirit of formal idiosyncrasy, a less obvious influence in succeeding works. Other interests include neglected figures of postwar modernism such as Gio Ponti, the abstract sculptures of Jorge Oteiza, Eduardo Chillida and Susana Solano, and contemporary cinema.

Der Abstand zwischen den Kanarischen Inseln und dem Rest Spaniens wird an den Arbeiten von Manuel Feo und seinen Mitarbeitern sichtbar, die mit dem im allgemeinen minimalistischen Ton ihrer Kollegen vom Festland brechen. Die rauhe Vulkanlandschaft der Inseln, die sich gewaltsam aus der Ruhe der horizontalen Meeresoberfläche erhebt, übertragen sie in die abgewinkelten Ebenen und gebrochenen Konturen ihrer Gebäude: Die unregelmäßigen Fenster und auskragenden Dachfensterblenden, die intensiven Farbflecken, die geneigten Fußböden, Rampen und gekrümmten Dächer, die um Wasserspeier, Traufleisten und ausladende Dachtraufen erweiterten Dachkonturen, die die Innenräume vor der vertikalen afrikanischen Sonne schützen.

Die pädagogische Hochschule der Universität von La Laguna war Feos erste bedeutende Arbeit mit Juan José Espino. Seit Anfang 1999 arbeitet er offiziell mit Victor Alonso zusammen, aber er arbeitet auch oft allein und mit anderen Architekten. Gegenwärtig baut er zusammen mit Elías Medina die El Pris Hermitage und andere religiöse Projekte auf Teneriffa. Feo beschreibt sein Architekturbüro als ein Laboratorium, das eine locker verbundene, an experimentellen Gestaltungen interessierte Gruppe von Architekten und Kunden anzieht.

Feo führt keine direkten Einflüsse an, aber seine Bezugspunkte unterscheiden sich von den Quellen, aus denen sich die Architektur des Festlands üblicherweise speist. Die pädagogische Hochschule schuldet etwas jenem Geist formaler Eigenart, der die Werke von Álvaro Siza charakterisiert, ein in späteren Werken weniger offensichtlicher Einfluß. Daneben lassen sich unter anderem vernachlässigte moderne Architekten der Nachkriegszeit wie Gio Ponti, die abstrakten Skulpturen von Jorge Oteiza, Eduardo Chillida und Susana Solano sowie das zeitgenössische Kino anführen.